EMPOWERMENT

For High Performing Organizations

"The essence of empowerment is optimizing performance, not simply delegating authority."

The Authors

D1372232

William A. Guillory and Linda A. Galindo

To Walt

with very warm regards

Bill 10/94

The cover design illustrates successive project cycles, beginning and ending at successive dots, represented by the solid line circles. After each cycle, expanded empowerment occurs as represented by the ΔEs.

Cover design by Lila Cazayoux

First Printing, 1995
ISBN: 0-933241-09-7
Printed in the United States of America

To Lea

Foreword

*The material in this book is primarily the result of our frustrations and successes in attempting to create an empowered organization. It is also the result of our 12 years of experience in assisting organizations, both in the U.S. and abroad, in facilitating the process of empowerment. The good news is the process works! The bad news is it is a long-term, challenging process. We believe that, no matter how challenging and difficult the process, empowerment is a necessity for the survival of most organizations around the world. In today's fast-paced, customer-oriented world, hierarchy simply does not work to meet the crucial expectations of **quality, speed, customization,** and **service**.*

This book is intended to clarify much of the mystery and confusion associated with empowerment. Replete with examples, you will undoubtedly begin to see yourself, your organization, and situations you can identify with in these pages. Slowly but surely, the magnitude and power of empowerment will be reinforced. "How to's" will be less necessary and your natural abilities and inclinations will take over.

This book is a journey. At first, like any uphill climb, you may seriously wonder if it is going to be worth it, or why you even started out in the first place. We encourage you to hang in there! From our own experience, when the fruits of your labor begin to manifest, there is no sweeter experience.

We come largely from our experience and we invite you to do the same. After all, that's what empowerment really is all about!

The Authors

INTRODUCTION

Empowerment is the capacity of an individual, a team, or an organization to perform. In this sense, empowerment will endure as a business or organizational performance requirement.

This text is divided into three major sections — *Personal and Organizational Empowerment, Teamwork,* and *Organizational Support System.* The first section defines empowerment, both in terms of the individual and the organization. It establishes the foundation upon which empowerment is based — personal responsibility, accountability, and empowerment. It further provides a three-step process for learning these crucial concepts as everyday working skills. The section concludes by discussing the relationship between personal empowerment and personal growth. We believe personal growth is at the heart of organizational transformation.

The second section is a discussion of teamwork and its importance to implementing *any* high employee involvement initiative. We attempt to show that teamwork is central to the success of empowerment, particularly in meeting the demand for speed in creating and delivering products, goods, and services. In this section, we discuss the definition of *team empowerment*, diversity in teams, and how to systematically incorporate teamwork. We also provide practical tools and exercises from our seminars that can be developed as practical working skills.

The third section is a discussion of the organizational support system necessary to have empowerment become institutionalized. We discuss three essential components — *leadership, management commitment,* and an *empowerment infrastructure.* The organizational support system requires leadership and commitment. The challenge is not only to one's self in giving up control and delegating authority, but also not allowing the effort to stall and die when the inevitable sources of resistance appear. For successful organizations, strong leadership is a necessity. For struggling organizations, the motivation is "we change or we go out of business." As you can surmise, the necessity for a new type of leader is emerging. One having courage and conviction to stay the course in a time of rapid and turbulent change *and* keep the organization successful!

This text is not intended to be an exhaustive treatise of empowerment. It is a discussion of philosophies, principles, and methodologies for implementing empowerment. Furthermore, based upon our experiences within our own organization and with clients, we know they work!

If you are a working practitioner of empowerment or high-involvement, then you can proceed to read the text in any way you find it most useful without having missed anything from previous chapters. Frankly, we like to skip around a book to get a feel for the message. On the other hand, if you are more methodical, then the discussion and application we believe are laid out in a logical manner.

We hope you gain value from and enjoy (in that order) our labor of love.

Bill Guillory
Linda Galindo

CONTENTS

PART III ORGANIZATIONAL SUPPORT SYSTEM

Innovations International, Inc.

Innovations is a global human resource development corporation specializing in personal and organizational transformation. We exist to provide the most advanced transformative technologies to corporations, globally, to assist them in prospering in the 1990s and into the 21st century.

Our specializations in consulting include:

- Diversity

- Empowerment

- Leadership

- Creativity

- Quantum-Thinking

These specializations include comprehensive consulting involving seminars, audits and assessments, coaching, and interactive multimedia learning.

For information regarding these offerings, please telephone, fax, or write:

Innovations International, Inc.
Woodlands Tower II
4021 South 700 East, Suite #650
Salt Lake City, Utah 84107
Tel (801) 268-3313
Fax (801) 268-3422

Acknowledgements

We acknowledge, most of all, our clients and employees who have taught us everything about this subject worth remembering and learning. We acknowledge our friends and colleagues who have contributed to this text in innumerable ways. One of the authors (William A. Guillory) would like to acknowledge his friend and mentor, Les Alberthal, as a constant source of inspiration and support in understanding the relationship between business and empowerment. Finally, we thank Melissa Egbert, who is really the managing editor of this manuscript. She has spent countless hours as the producer in bringing this text to reality. Thanks!

I. PERSONAL AND ORGANIZATIONAL EMPOWERMENT

"There is no such thing as an empowered organization, without competent, self-managed, and continuously-learning employees."

The Authors

CHAPTER ONE

EMPOWERMENT

As the CEO of Data Systems, Inc. delivered his state of the company address to the work force, his audience became visibly more attentive when he made his final pronouncement "Competition is demanding that we change the way things are done. We are committed to our quality initiative and you are key to our success. You are empowered to do whatever it takes for us to be successful."

Harry, who had joined the company a year ago, thought "I wish you'd tell my manager that. I see a lot of things that could help this organization and if I offer even so much as a suggestion, I'm told it's always been done this way. If I try to rock the boat one more time, I'll be lucky to keep my job."

- Does the CEO need to clarify what he means by ". . .you are empowered. . .?"
- Is Harry's manager the problem?
- Does Harry have anything to do with the conflict he is experiencing with his manager?

What does *empowerment* mean anyway?

Before attempting to describe how an organizational initiative such as empowerment is implemented and institutionalized, it is vitally important to define empowerment. In order to do so, we would first like to describe the *contextual model* shown below:

{CONTEXT}	{CONTENT}	{EXPERIENCE}
Environment	**Structure and System**	**Process**

1

Context characterizes the environment or climate. It is usually described by a vision statement:

> *"Innovations is a highly-competent, self-managed and continuously-learning organization."*

Context is a description of "what it is (or could be) like" to work in a given organization, i.e., "the people in this organization are supportive and fun to work with." Leadership often communicates from this domain.

Content characterizes the description of the management structure and system, i.e., a flat structure and a high employee involvement system. Management operates and communicates most often from this domain. It is a description of "what is done" in order to implement the new initiative.

Experience characterizes the process of implementing an initiative by putting processes and procedures into practice. Most employees operate from this domain by posing the question, "How do I (we) do it?"

North American Semiconductors, Inc. experienced a shift to global competition almost overnight. To remain competitive, it was clear to the leadership that a new way had to be implemented to meet customer demands faster than the competition, while ensuring quality products.

Taking time out to examine the situation, the CEO came to some very clear conclusions to produce a return on stockholder investment. These conclusions would dictate future communication to her leadership team and to the organization:

- I must clearly describe what I see is our future, and communicate it frequently. Within that description I must elaborate on what it will be like to work here in that future. (Context)

> **The Vision:** An innovative, flexible organization focused on business processes which are responsive to exceeding customer needs, and
>   - Characterized by mutual respect, personal integrity, open communication, and trust.
>   - Employees who have a passion for service, learning, and continuous improvement.
>
> - This future dictates that we operate in a more empowered way. Management requires an understanding of, and the ability to implement this way of operating. (Content)
>
> **The Principles:** A structure and system which,
>   - Are organized around our customers as the focus of our business processes.
>   - Are organized for speed and responsiveness.
>   - Shift from management to support and facilitation.
>   - Support competence driven participative leadership.
>
> - I will tap into the knowledge and experience of this organization to best understand how to achieve the new vision. I will create a way for everyone to be involved in helping me understand "how we do it." (Experience)
>
> **The Process:** We must,
>   - Focus on processes which create customer partnerships.
>   - Benchmark relative to the best that exist as a standard to creatively exceed.
>   - Encourage, acknowledge, and reward outstanding individual and team performances.
>   - Model, foster, and live individual and collective responsibility and accountability in everything we do.

With these descriptions in mind, we can now define empowerment in a way which incorporates the function of each domain.

Empowerment is an organizational context which fosters and encourages the *optimum performance* of its employees, both individually and as teams,

which is implemented by

a system of high employee involvement within a *decentralized* organizational structure,

with employees

who progressively assume greater *responsibility* and *accountability* for their jobs through *continuous-learning*.

This definition of empowerment has three key elements:

1) The expectation of optimum individual and team performance.

2) A high employee involvement system within a decentralized structure.

3) Self-motivated employees who are committed to continuous-learning.

Notice the focus is on *maximizing human potential* and *optimizing performance*.

Achieving a more empowered organization requires the complementary efforts of a committed Organizational Support System and employees having a high degree of Individual and Team Empowerment. Individual and Team Empowerment refers to competent employees whose performance justifies the delegation of job authority within clearly defined guidelines. Therefore, the basic unit necessary to implement empowerment is competent, continuously learning employees.

The systematic process of implementing empowerment is illustrated by the following diagram:

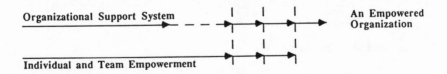

Empowerment

When most (hierarchical) organizations begin an empowerment initiative, the ability of the work force to perform independently is typically greater than the authority they have been delegated. This difference is illustrated by the differing lengths of the two solid arrows above. The difference in the lengths of the two arrows, indicated by the dotted portion, represents the extent to which employees can competently perform, but are not delegated authority to do so. Therefore, when delegation is initially the major implementation activity, individuals and teams are being delegated tasks which they can already accomplish. When the two solid lines become equal in length, the empowerment process begins in earnest.

> The results of an empowerment assessment at a local publishing company revealed that the work force was capable of more than they were being allowed to do. Counterproductive work force behaviors including high absenteeism, an unwillingness to participate in organizational meetings, and "just getting by," now had an explanation. Recently, management had focused on the message to reduce costs and improve efficiency. Management stressed the importance of individual initiative in continuous-learning, working together with less necessity for being managed, and becoming more decentralized. Everyone began in earnest to carry out the new mandates, but when the time came for some individual managers to really "let go" where people were able to perform, they were finding it more difficult than they thought it would be.

The process of moving toward greater organizational empowerment is progressively delegating expanded responsibility (Organizational Support System, top arrow) and having individuals and teams successfully achieve that level of expanded delegation (Individual and Team Empowerment, bottom arrow). Responsible delegation means assigning a project or task to an individual or a team, within clearly defined guidelines, at or beyond their level of *demonstrated* ability to perform (top dashed arrows).

Delegation beyond demonstrated ability to perform, by definition, will correspondingly require new learning, both in terms of mindset and skills on the part of leadership, management, and employees. Leadership and management will be required to provide mentoring, coaching, support, and the sharing of power and control. Employees will be required to continuously learn new skills and information, how to manage and organize their jobs, and to *expand* their sense of responsibility and accountability for their work (lower dashed arrows). This is the *essence* of the progressive application of the top and bottom dashed arrows in the diagram.

For example, in the implementation of its empowerment initiative, the ENSERCH Corporation developed the following guidelines for its leaders (Organizational Support System) and its employees (Individual and Team Empowerment).

Empowerment exists when:

LEADERS

- Delegate sufficient authority for employees to do their jobs and satisfy their customers' requirements.

- Communicate standards for employee performance and require performance against such standards.

- Encourage and make available skill development and training.

EMPLOYEES

- Accept the responsibility to perform their jobs to the best of their abilities and to satisfy their customers' requirements.

- Accept the responsibility to achieve or surpass the performance standards for their jobs.

- Achieve their full potential by developing the skills to fully perform their responsibilities.

Empowerment

- Provide a supportive environment and constructive performance coaching.

- Seek and value employee input on both work processes and broader issues.

- Encourage informed risk-taking and proactive decision-making, accepting honest mistakes without reprisal.

- Provide input on work processes and broader issues.

- Act as part of an overall company team and support the decisions of that team.

- Develop a sense of personal ownership of the business.

These guidelines illustrate how the two complementary components of an empowered organization play out in terms of process.

Figure 1 is a description of the continuum which exists between hierarchical and self-management styles of operation. Superimposing the diagram shown on page 4 on Figure 1 implies that empowerment is best implemented in progressive steps corresponding to "responsible delegation" and "continuous-learning." The extent to which an organization moves along this scale from left to right will be determined by the necessities of the business market, the commitment of leadership, and ultimately the willingness of the work force to accept, by performance, this new reality.

MODELS OF MANAGEMENT

**HIERARCHICAL
MODEL**

Vertical Organization
Systems Oriented
Individual Oriented
Management/Supervision
Job Focused/Fixed

**SELF-MANAGEMENT
MODEL**

Horizontal Organization
People Oriented
Interdependence Oriented
Mentorship/Coaching
Job Flexible/Changing

← Management Orientation   High-Involvement Orientation →

———— **Organizational Empowerment** ————→

Figure 1. Hierarchical Self-Management Continuum

8

CHAPTER TWO

THE EMPOWERED ORGANIZATION

Given the definition of empowerment in the previous chapter, an empowered organization is one which has *integrated* the practice of high-involvement with management operation (Figure 1). In the sense of diversity, the organization utilizes the entire spectrum of operation represented by Figure 1, although the overwhelming majority of operation is strongly shifted to the right side. For U.S. and Western-oriented organizations, this integration process is not only practical, but realistic. Given the necessities of a *totally* empowered organization (extreme right of Figure 1) — total employee ownership and performance — it is unrealistic and possibly unnecessary for most organizations to operate in this manner. All employees do not necessarily want the degree of personal change and personal responsibility necessary to operate in a totally empowered manner — either individually or as teams.

Gerald was growing more frustrated by the day. Very few of his co-workers seemed to be practicing what they had learned in their empowerment training. "This is great stuff," he thought. "Why is everyone still blaming management? The responsibility is ours to change things." At lunch Gerald stopped a negative and counterproductive conversation by asking how he could help the situation. He knew it annoyed his co-workers but he was unwilling to pass up the opportunity to take ownership and improve what he could. Over time, Gerald realized some individuals would find it difficult to change. He decided not to use them as his excuse not to continue on his own personal empowerment journey.

The real objective of empowerment is posed by the question, "How far do we have to move, as an organization, along the diagram in Figure 1, in order to be a high performance organization?" If 70% is the answer, then, on average, the organizational operation should be an integration of 70% high-involvement orientation and 30% management orientation. If the answer is 40%, the operation should be 40% high-involvement orientation and 60% management orientation, where management and high-involvement orientations refer to the left and right sides of Figure 1, respectively. By using this integrated approach, an organization has available the entire spectrum of operation, and the flexibility to use the most effective approach as a function of the situation. In other words, some degree of management is not only necessary, but in some cases, desirable.

Since high performance is the desired end, "How do we define such a globally competitive organization?" A high performance organization is one which has successfully integrated Teamwork, Quality, Work Process Redesign (Reengineering), Environment, Safety & Health (ES&H), Diversity, and Empowerment as shown in Figure 2.

Diversity spans each of the vertical initiatives by virtue of the employees performing them and the full array of differences they inherently bring to the process. Empowerment is the foundation upon which each of these initiatives is based, in practice, since they all require high employee involvement. Each of these initiatives also requires, as a necessity, personally empowered employees. A personally empowered employee is a self-motivated individual who consistently performs to a high degree of his or her capability, within an organizationally supportive framework.

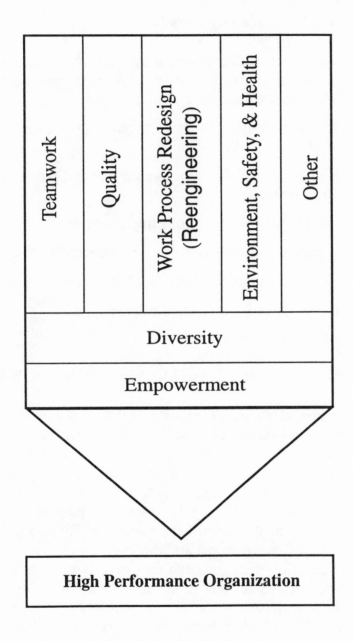

Figure 2. The Integrated Initiatives of a
High Performance Organization

A High Performance Organization

Empowerment serves as the integrating initiative for achieving a high performance organization. A high performance organization has the following characteristics:

1) Customer-focused — assures *quality, customization, speed,* and *service.*

2) Operates in a highly empowered manner, individually and as teams.

3) Institutionalizes continuous improvement.

4) Receptive and responsive to, and anticipates change.

5) Capitalizes on its diversity as a competitive advantage.

6) Is knowledge-based and continuously-learning.

7) Is globally competitive.

Each of these characteristics will be discussed, in turn, below.

The four key elements of a *customer-focused* organization have been discussed by Harry S. Dent, Jr.[1] — they are quality, customization, speed, and service. We suggest that these are also the crucial requirements for surviving, as a business, in the 1990s. In order to operate with these four elements, an organization will require highly competent employees who have the freedom to perform their responsibilities with the least amount of management and direction — *high employee involvement.* Solutions, in large part, will have to originate with those closest to the problems. Employee-customer partnerships will have to be encouraged wherever practical and/or sensible. Such a partnership serves as the basis for *continuous improvement* of products, goods, and services from the established customer feedback relationship.

Superimposed upon continuously changing customer demands is the fact that these requirements and the processes necessary to produce them are changing almost monthly; and in some cases, daily. We live and work in a period where *change* is so rapid and unpredictable that we have to learn to become comfortable with chaos and ambiguity. That is, we must be simultaneously receptive and responsive to change, and then learn to anticipate it by being on the leading edge of change. A profound element of recent change is the recognition of the value of *diversity*, particularly since the world's work force and customer base are diverse.

Diversity-thinking provides the opportunity for higher quality decision-making, problem-solving, innovation, and creativity as compared to homogeneous-thinking. Thus, diversity has the potential to be a significant competitive advantage. In a *knowledge-based* era, competitive advantage can only be maintained where there is continuous-learning. The seventh characteristic is the recognition that corporations compete in a borderless, *global economy*. Customers can acquire any product or service, of the highest quality, from anywhere in the world. Taken together as an integrated way of functioning, these seven (7) characteristics define a high performance organization.

Empowerment Requires Fundamental Change

The reason empowerment is so challenging is that we must not only change the way we organize and perform work, but we must also *fundamentally change* our traditional beliefs, attitudes, and assumptions about work. Such fundamental change is more accurately defined as personal and organizational transformation.

Empowerment requires transformation of our fundamental beliefs about:

1) Personal responsibility and accountability

2) Performance

3) Self-motivated continuous-learning

4) Value-added employment

5) Self-management

6) Individualism

7) Change

8) Leadership

Each of these topics will be discussed in terms of how our attitudes will have to change in order for empowerment to work.

1) **Personal Responsibility and Accountability** — In order for expanded responsible delegation to occur, employees will have to assume greater charge of their work tasks. They will have to plan with greater care and knowledge, anticipate pitfalls, and design solutions in advance. In the end, personal accountability means ownership of the results — successful and unsuccessful — without any reasons or excuses. This attitude provides the basis for new learning when the results are unsuccessful.

2) **Performance** — Empowerment will force us to encounter and move beyond self-imposed limitations about our capabilities to perform. The greatest challenge we face in expanding our performance is not in learning new skills, but our strongly held *beliefs* about what we should or should not be required to do in this new high-involvement environment. What we will have to learn and accept is that we should change in whatever way necessary (within moral and ethical bounds) to exceed our customers' expectations — both internal and external.

3) **Self-Motivated Continuous-learning** — In the present knowledge-based era, continuous-learning is a necessity. Without continuous-learning, an employee jeopardizes her or his value to an organization. In high-involvement organizations, greater personal responsibility means the individual is self-motivated to acquire new learning by being in constant contact with the continuously changing needs of customers.

4) **Value-Added Employment** — This requirement principally involves a shift in mindset from entitlement to "my employment is based upon the continuing value I bring to internal or external customers. In essence, I do not work for a company, I work for a customer. I have the highest probability for secure employment when I exceed my identified customer's expectations. This mode of thinking allows me to accurately define value-added work."

5) **Self-Management** — Again, a natural consequence of expanded delegation with less oversight is the necessity for each employee to assume management responsibilities previously performed by his or her

manager. It is important to realize that management does not disappear, it is simply passed on to the employee. A crucial aspect of this new responsibility is the ability to organize and prioritize one's work independently. In the initial stages, coaching and mentoring may be necessary.

6) **Individualism** — This requirement is probably the most difficult of all for many Western-oriented individuals — those primarily motivated by individual self-interest. It involves a fundamental shift to authentically value and practice, without pretense, teamwork. It requires the realization that business competitiveness and success, in the future, will be a balance of synergistic group interdependence *and* the full expression of individual excellence.

7) **Change** — This element principally involves adopting a mindset that rapid change is a way of life. What appears to be chaos and confusion, because so many things are happening simultaneously, is the new norm. It is the acceptance of a mindset that an employee's job is a continuously changing function of what internal and external customers want and need. And that such change is created by unpredictable events referred to as chaos. The key here is to relinquish the necessity for personal control or security.

8) **Leadership** — Empowering leadership involves the continual process of creating expanded competence and giving away responsibility. It is a shift from an individually-led mindset to a comprehensive participative leadership mindset. Therefore, leadership exists at every level of an organization. Its focus is on establishing a high standard of excellence and inspiring

employees to self-enroll in committing to achieve that level of performance.

Empowerment in Action

The crucial requirement for the success of empowerment is that the individual employee must fulfill the delegated authority through a strong sense of self-accountability. An outstanding example of an organization which makes this fundamental assumption of all of its employees is W.L. Gore and Associates, Inc. in Flagstaff, Arizona. This corporation assumes that if you treat people as responsible adults, they will respond as such in turn. This is one of the most important principles upon which this organization was based since its founding in the late 1950s.

As an example, when a new technical employee joins Gore, she or he is encouraged to discuss projects with a number of working groups in order to decide how she or he might bring the greatest value to the organization rather than have the organization make an outright job assignment. In this way, the organization fosters employee ownership and commitment to its goals. This obvious, yet powerful, assumption is the basis for the high degree of empowerment and success their employees experience individually and as a corporation. This is an example of an organization which has chosen to operate at the far right side of Figure 1. Every organization should make a similar choice based upon its unique work force and customer requirements.

Simultaneously, with this focus on the individual is an interdependent network of individuals and organizational units that *require* each other's contribution for their individual and collective success. For example, in a consulting firm an

17

individual in Research and Development may come up with a brilliant idea for a sales presentation. However, by the time it is delivered to a client audience, it has involved computer (and graphic) specialists, sales and marketing personnel, scheduling, materials disbursement, sales presentation arrangements, and finally the individual who makes the presentation. Without the cooperation and self-accountability of each of these units, the delivery of that presentation to a client audience would lack total quality service in some way. Even though the individual making the presentation might appear to be the star, each individual and group involved in that process are equally stars. In an empowered organization, they are genuinely valued and acknowledged as such.

Having established an understanding of empowerment and its fundamental role in creating a high performance organization, we can now proceed to discuss the fundamental principles upon which empowerment is based.

CHAPTER THREE

THE PRINCIPLES OF EMPOWERMENT

The principles of empowerment define the structure, guidelines, and functions governing how empowerment is to be implemented.

1) ***People are an organization's most important resource.***

   The *most important principle of empowerment is that people are more important than management systems.* Although projects may come and go, the most vital recyclable resource in the entire picture, which is utilized over and over again, is people. This realization leads to understanding the absolute necessity to preserve the mental, physical, emotional, and even the spiritual well-being of employees. In the present progression from information-oriented businesses to knowledge-based businesses, the development, utilization, and retention of creative employees may well determine the survival of an organization.

2) ***High-involvement is maximized.***

   The fundamental assumption of high-involvement is that the more employees are involved in designing and controlling their work functions, the more productively and efficiently the organization will operate. For high-involvement to work, employees must assume responsibility and accountability for understanding and ensuring the successful production of a "whole aspect of work." Individually and collectively, employees must have a high degree of self-discipline and self-management in order to operate with the least amount of oversight or management. The crucial fact to understand is that in today's hyper-accelerated world, high-involvement is inevitable.

3) *Teamwork is valued and rewarded.*

Teamwork has three major advantages: 1) A whole aspect of a product or service which involves several or many parts (steps) can be performed continuously in the most efficient and effective manner by a team, 2) Teams provide the opportunity for synergism which is not possible for an individual working alone, and 3) Team functioning, over a sustained period, maximizes the overall health and well-being of employees. Empowered teams have two vital elements: 1) The full expression of individual excellence, and 2) The necessity (or preference) for interdependence in order to achieve the team goal. When this principle is applied to the organization, the organization is viewed as a network of interdependent centers of excellence where the focus of commitment of these business units must be balanced with commitment to the overall success of the organization.

4) *Personal and professional growth are continuous.*

Personal growth and professional development are *a way of life in empowered organizations.* Since empowerment is a *dynamic process* rather than a specific goal to be reached, there is the sequential cycle of self-motivated goal setting and achievement, which continually drives the enhanced capability of employees (pg 4). High-involvement necessitates people-oriented skills, hence the corresponding necessity for continual personal growth. This principle is also one which makes a job interesting, fun, and creative because of its continuous improvement nature.

5) *Responsibility and accountability are maximized.*

Empowerment is based upon maximizing individual and collective responsibility and accountability. This means a predisposed mindset of total responsibility for projects or tasks which are delegated. Such a mindset has the potential for not only meeting, but exceeding, customer or client expectations. Without a critical fraction of highly responsible and accountable employees, empowerment is not possible. The more difficult of these two requirements is holding self and others accountable. Accountability is probably *the* limiting factor in determining the extent to which high-involvement is possible.

6) *Self-determination, self-motivation, and self-management are expected.*

An inherent assumption of empowerment is that most, if not all, employees have the talent and capability to perform their jobs and responsibilities with the least amount of direction. Where the talent or capability is lacking, principle (4) above applies. An additional assumption is that the incentive to meet (and possibly exceed) job expectations comes from within an individual. Given principles (4) and (5) above and a clear organizational support system, employees are expected to be self-driven in terms of determination, motivation, and management.

7) *Expanded delegation is a continual process.*

It is vitally important to understand that the act of delegation is not empowerment. The procedure for *implementing* empowerment is delegation of responsibility within clearly defined guidelines. Empowerment ultimately depends most on an individual's ability to perform the expanded responsibility which has been delegated. A requirement of expanded delegation is to ensure that an individual or a team is maximally prepared to accept the expanded responsibility. The central issue which is crucial to the success of empowerment is giving up "control." This process requires trust and the willingness to share information, knowledge, and power. The continual question a manager asks himself or herself in an empowering environment is, "How do I mentor and coach what I do, and give it away?" Therefore, mentoring and coaching become critical management skills in support of delegation.

8) *Hierarchy is minimized.*

A natural consequence of extensive delegation is the systematic reduction of hierarchy. Hierarchical organizational structures discourage empowerment by supporting a "line-of-authority" system and discouraging cross-functional teams. Cross-functional teams focus on clients or customers, products, goods, or services. This principle, in an indirect way, means that influence and authority are sourced in *demonstrated* competence, performance, and an ability to provide what is wanted and needed, rather than solely on position power.

9) *Organizational leadership and support are necessary to drive and sustain empowerment.*

> Empowerment cannot exist without a clear commitment from the organizational leadership. Leadership must communicate the necessity or desirability for empowerment and link it to the organization's opportunity for greater success. The support system involves the systematic change in processes, procedures, structures, and a redesign in the way work is done, i.e., greater emphasis on teamwork. The simplest way to express this principle is that leadership and management must *live* the empowerment vision and *model* the values by putting into visible practice what is preached.

The ultimate objective of management by empowerment is to realize that the more able and capable everyone becomes in terms of self-responsibility and self-accountability, the less necessity there is to oversee, supervise, or manage employees.

These principles provide the context within which empowerment can be practiced, depending on the nature of the organization and its traditional culture. Next, we discuss the foundation upon which empowerment is based in practice.

CHAPTER FOUR

THE FOUNDATION OF EMPOWERMENT

The practice of empowerment is founded upon a clear experiential understanding *and* acceptance of three important concepts: *personal responsibility, personal accountability,* and *personal empowerment.* For example, when a manager or team coordinator delegates authority for a certain project, what is the assumed agreement when she or he says, "I am holding you accountable for the results of this project?" What does it mean when a team assumes responsibility and accountability for the performance of a project in a given time frame? Answers to these questions become clear when there is a clear understanding of these concepts. We will discuss each of them, in-depth, in the following sections.

Personal Responsibility

Personal responsibility is the willingness to view yourself as the *principal source* of the results and circumstances which occur in your life, both individually and collectively with others in the workplace.

This is a challenging requirement. However, it is based upon the experiential observation of life as it exists, not upon the assumption that life should be fair. The emphasis in this definition is on creating a mindset which focuses on producing results in the most proactive manner, without the excess expenditure of time, work, or energy. Managers and employees are most effective in coaching those areas, i.e., interpersonal skills, leadership, continuous-learning, etc., which they have personally mastered and claim maximum personal responsibility for themselves. In a like manner, we are least effective in those areas for which we have been marginally personally responsible.

In the definition of personal responsibility above, *principal source* can be as great or as little as you choose. There is no restriction as to how responsible you believe you are for the results which occur in your life, *as a predisposed mindset.* You can just as easily believe you are 90% responsible as you can believe you are 50% responsible. However, the results consistently produced over time by each of these mindsets are vastly different. The 90% individual accomplishes most, if not all, of the goals he or she establishes, whereas the 50% individual, in general, has a constant array of reasons and excuses why he or she did not succeed.

Personal Accountability

Personal accountability is the willingness to *claim ownership* for the results which are produced as a consequence of your involvement, both individually and collectively with others in the workplace.

The key word in this definition is *ownership*. If we assume ownership for whatever occurs, we can take charge of initiating the appropriate action. If we abdicate accountability, then we feel powerless to take action. Therefore, outside assistance is necessary to initiate positive change in our behalf. Furthermore, the extent to which managers and employees can proactively hold others accountable is directly proportional to the extent to which they assume personal responsibility. Thus, responsibility and accountability are complementary sides of the same coin. Through ownership of the difficulties as well as the successes in the workplace, the truly successful manager or employee recognizes the opportunity for feedback, growth, and the acquisition of new skills in the areas where deficiencies exist.

In order to acquire a quantitative sense of these concepts, we have developed a Responsibility Scale, shown as Figure 3. This scale is based upon a very important assumption: *Every individual has available 100% personal responsibility for the events which occur in his or her life, as a theoretical limit.* The scale shown as Figure 3a is representative of an individual who assumes he or she is, on the average, 50% personally responsible and therefore 50% personally accountable. *If* the assumption of 100% *availability* is valid, then this individual abdicates 50% responsibility and he or she feels victimized and disempowered to influence those events.

The illustration shown as Figure 3b is for an individual who assumes 70% personal responsibility, on the average, for the events which occur in her or his life. We can see how the victim-disempowered area is diminished relative to the responsible-accountable area. Figure 3c illustrates an individual whose predisposed assumption of personal responsibility is 90%. This mindset is indicative of an individual who achieves, on the average, most of his or her established goals in life. The top scale in this figure has the phrase Personal Empowerment. Thus, we can begin to understand that the most important requirement for personal empowerment is the assumption of a high degree of personal responsibility and accountability. The relationship between these three vitally important concepts is summarized by the

RESPONSIBILITY SCALE

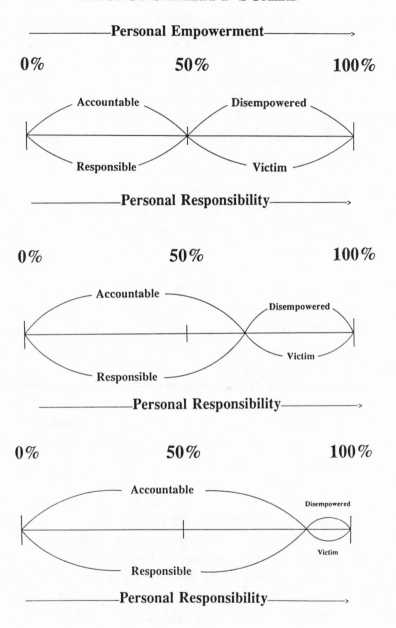

Figure 3. Personal Responsibility and Accountability
Represented on a 0 to 100% Scale

28

following statement: *An individual is personally empowered only to the extent he or she assumes a predisposed mindset of personal responsibility and accountability.*

The announcement of an empowerment initiative in Julio's organization brought great excitement. Based on their understanding of it, many employees felt it was long overdue. For too long, managers who were too far removed from the actual work had controlled how work was organized. Julio hoped that this would mean that the dictator-like manager over his department would be ousted, or get the message and leave.

To his surprise, the first training Julio was offered had to do with becoming a personally empowered, self-motivated, continuously-learning employee! "As usual, they want more out of me," Julio thought. "When are they going to do something about these managers?!" As the training progressed he realized that "management control" wasn't necessarily the problem. Through realistic case studies he learned that no matter what, he was responsible and accountable for the results he produced. It was hard to understand at first.

Over time, the scapegoats for lack of individual production began falling away and the organization was slowly putting in a support system for the new learning. His manager is still over the department and has become much more of a resource than a barrier. Julio realized his manager was not the only one who underwent new learning.

Personal Empowerment

Personal empowerment is an *internally-derived* capacity to perform at or above an established level of expectation. It is expanded by going beyond both self-imposed and external limitations through continuous-learning.

Personal empowerment is the dynamic process of systematically invalidating self-imposed beliefs *and* organizational barriers which serve to limit exceptional performance. If one's ability to perform comes from within, it means that no one can personally empower someone else with the ability to perform. It also means that the act of delegation is not empowerment, but *is* a vitally important mode of operation in the achievement of an empowered organization.

For example, an employee may strongly believe that he or she should not have to compete on an uneven playing field. If that belief serves to limit his or her performance, then it is self-imposed, regardless of the fact that the playing field may, in fact, be uneven. The question is, "What do I do now with the circumstances that presently exist, while the organization and certain key individuals are working to 'level the playing field?'" Although this is a question that each individual has to answer for himself or herself, an empowering suggestion would be to use every opportunity to further personal and professional growth, confident in the fact that you are preparing yourself for your personal goal. Whether it is with your present organization or another that is more receptive to your advancement and success.

In a like manner, another employee may feel victimized and stymied by certain actions on the part of the organization to create a level playing field. This is an example of an apparent external limitation for that individual. Sometimes, such actions are referred to as "reverse discrimination." The recommendation to an empowered individual is to accept the fact that real, level competition from traditionally underutilized segments of the organization will be the way of the future. A new element in the promotion and advancement process will be a committed effort that *no one* will be denied advancement because of race, color, sex, religion, sexual orientation, national origin, etc. *and* that concrete steps in assessment and planning will be taken to ensure this commitment. When this reality is non-reactively accepted, it will be realized that such a commitment benefits *everyone* in the long run. The employee is challenged to take this new reality into consideration as he or she plans a career strategy rather than focusing on the unfairness of the situation.

Eugene's world was changing faster than he could cope. Last month it was some "diversity thing" they all had to go to and tomorrow the "right sizing" plan would be announced. He had been in line for a much awaited promotion and now the chances seemed minimal that it would come through. Why wasn't Mark rattled? Nothing seemed to faze him. He even walked off right in the middle of a complaint session by a group of employees, and he had every right to be angry. A woman got the supervisor's job that should have been his!

When Eugene had a chance to talk things over with Mark, the response surprised him. "It's a new world, we have to pay attention and prepare. Janet deserved the job and I, for one, plan to help make her successful. Anything less and I'd be hurting my own future opportunities. The diversity initiative makes sense. I'll plan a new strategy for my success and be ready for whatever comes. Just because I can't control what's happening in our work environment doesn't mean I'm not responsible for my own success." Eugene walked away thinking "Maybe he understands something I don't."

Understanding personal empowerment and how it becomes a learned skill is crucial to implementing management by empowerment. It is equally important to understand that someone cannot personally empower someone else; empowerment comes from within. However, through the establishment of a relationship based upon *mutual respect, trust,* and *equality,* it becomes possible to mentor or coach the proactive empowerment of an employee, a team member, or a co-worker.

The Empowered Individual

In the discussion above, we established that the extent to which an individual is personally empowered is measured by

31

her or his demonstrated ability to perform. Therefore, personal characteristics (i.e., self-motivation) drive natural and learned competencies to generate professional performance, as shown in Figure 4. Personal characteristics are primarily an indication of an individual's mindset. In an overall sense, it characterizes the extent to which an individual is personally driven, *from within*, to succeed in spite of the situation or circumstances. Most successful people believe that this component is the more important of this two-component model. Education and skills are also vitally important in determining the performance of an individual. The greater the knowledge and skill, the more *potentially* exceptional the individual's performance. Thus, merely having a degree from a prestigious academic institution (even with a high GPA) does not ensure a highly productive employee over the course of a career. In a like manner, an individual from a lesser known institution (with a strong GPA) may actually perform in an exceptional manner over the course of a career; particularly if traditional systemic barriers of elitism are removed and *all* employees are encouraged to perform to the full extent of their self-driven abilities.

The following set of guidelines are designed to assist you in systematically and proactively expanding your personal empowerment:

1) *Assess your present level of personal empowerment.*

    Honestly evaluate your present level of personal and professional mastery of your job by soliciting input from a broad spectrum of sources.

THE EMPOWERED INDIVIDUAL

PERSONALITY CHARACTERISTICS	NATURAL AND LEARNED COMPETENCIES
Dedication	Education
Persistence	Skills
Commitment	Talents
Self-Motivation	Abilities
Self-Responsibility	Strengths

$$\left\{ \text{Personality Characteristics} \right\} \rightarrow \left\{ \text{Natural and Learned Competencies} \right\} \rightarrow \left\{ \text{Professional Performance} \right\}$$

Figure 4. Personal Characteristics drive Natural and Learned Competencies, which result in an individual's measurable Performance.

2) *Determine whether your performance falls below, meets, or exceeds customer expectations.*

Assess the quality of your performance through the eyes of your internal/external customer.

3) *If your performance is below expectations, assess your level of commitment.*

If your performance is below expectations and you are sufficiently skilled for your present job, seriously re-examine if you are committed to meeting the expectations of your present job. If not, make plans for doing something else.

4) *If committed, determine the new skills you require.*

If you feel you are committed to meeting the expectations of your present job, write, in detail, the new personal and/or professional skills you require (with the help of a mentor, if necessary), based upon expanded responsibility and accountability.

5) *Acquire a mentor/coach to hold you accountable.*

Acquire a mentor or a coach to assist you and hold you accountable to your commitment, based upon the consistent results you produce.

6) *Overcome your self-limitations.*

When you encounter a barrier, have your mentor facilitate you in overcoming it. Remember, it is ultimately *your* responsibility to take charge of invalidating your self-limiting belief(s) by designing and performing non-comfort zone actions.

7) *If committed to expanded empowerment, define a new challenging area of activity.*

If you meet or exceed your present job expectations, describe a project or an area of activity which you would enjoy and involves significantly expanded responsibility in terms of the acquisition of new personal and/or professional skills.

8) *Proceed and apply (5) and (6) where difficulties occur.*

Begin the project, utilizing and/or learning proven professional methods and knowledge. If difficulties or problems occur, apply steps 5) and 6) above.

In the next chapter, we discuss processes for having personal responsibility, accountability, and empowerment become functional skills in the workplace.

CHAPTER FIVE

LEARNING FUNDAMENTAL EMPOWERMENT SKILLS

We indicated at the beginning of the previous chapter that implementing empowerment requires an experiential understanding and acceptance of personal responsibility, accountability, and empowerment. The first exercise in this chapter is designed to accomplish this objective. To have these three concepts become functional skills requires application and practice of the internalized definitions. The second exercise in this chapter is designed to accomplish this objective.

The Network is Down — An Empowerment Exercise

This exercise can be done alone or, preferably, with a group of not more than six (6) participants. The exercise begins with each participant declaring to what extent, on a 0 to 100% scale, she or he believes the following quote:

> *"Individuals carry their success or their*
> *failure with them . . . it does not*
> *depend on outside conditions . . ."*

> **Ralph Waldo Trine**

Example: "I believe 70% of my success depends on me and 30% on outside conditions."

Instructions:

1) Read the story on the following page (pg 39).

2) Complete the True/False quiz alone (pg 40).

3) Through discussion, reach a "group consensus*" regarding each of the True/False statements within your assigned group. The discussion time is limited to one hour.

4) Select someone in the group to record your group rationale for each True/False group answer (pg 41).

* **Group consensus** is the collective agreement of the group, which includes the minority opinion as an integrated part of the group decision.

THE NETWORK IS DOWN!

The leadership of an Information Management Corporation decides to aggressively incorporate an Empowerment Initiative throughout the organization to complement their ongoing quality program. Managers are asked to delegate more authority to employees and to create teams across divisions. One of the more enterprising teams designs an interdivisional communications network system. The team insists on working independently, with little or no input from management. The network system also bypasses most of the previous decision-making authority of the team members' direct managers. During the design phase, team members complain of unnecessary bureaucracy and a lack of critical and timely information flow from management. The direct managers, who previously had strict guidelines for information dissemination, have no new guidelines from the senior leadership on what information can be distributed. When the new system is initially made operational, breakdown occurs. After the system is restored and functioning for three months, it is evaluated to be less efficient and less cost-effective than the previous communication system. The senior leadership promises to make a decision regarding the continuation of the team project after studying the evaluation.

Based on the story, circle the following choices as True (T) or False (F).

1) The interdivisional team members were   T   F
    each personally responsible for the
    system breakdown.

2) The direct managers were responsible for   T   F
    ensuring the success of the
    interdivisional team.

3) To some degree, management control of   T   F
    employees is necessary.

4) Supervision is unnecessary for an   T   F
    employee who feels he or she is
    personally empowered.

5) The direct managers were responsible   T   F
    and accountable for providing the
    necessary information to the team.

6) The senior leadership was not committed   T   F
    to the Empowerment Initiative.

7) The direct managers were accountable   T   F
    for the system breakdown irrespective of
    whether or not their input was included.

8) The senior leadership was 100%   T   F
    responsible and 100% accountable for
    the entire situation.

THE NETWORK IS DOWN!

A Group Decision-Making Exercise

Please record a brief statement of the rationale of your group in reaching consensus.

1)   T   F :

2)   T   F :

3)   T   F :

4)   T   F :

5)   T   F :

6)   T   F :

7)   T   F :

8)   T   F :

Summary of important empowerment principles raised in this case study:

1) Incorporating empowerment requires much more (i.e., an infrastructure) than a directive from the senior leadership.

2) The establishment of basic principles and definitions of empowerment organization-wide is necessary for the successful implementation of empowerment.

3) Middle managers (with vast experience, knowledge, and skills) are crucial to the success of empowerment.

4) The change process requires expanded interpersonal and negotiation skills to have a smooth transition.

5) Instituting a new culture (and system) will almost invariably be less efficient and less productive in the short run, particularly where education and training are not provided.

6) Commitment is typically measured by how decisively leadership responds when a difficulty (or crisis) occurs.

When the performance of a team is limited or severely hampered because of resistance to necessary (and inevitable) change, then it is difficult, if not impossible, to implement organizational empowerment.

Each True/False statement in the exercise on page 40 was designed to bring out an operational principle of empowerment. If we base our criteria for each True or False answer on the opportunity for professional development, teamwork, and organizational productivity, then the following answers and operational principles become vitally important for empowered performance.

THE NETWORK IS DOWN!

Operational Principles for Empowerment

1) **True** Principle: Each team member is simultaneously 100% responsible for his or her unique participation and 100% responsible for the results produced by the team. This principle establishes a truly unique paradigm of performance and achievement.

2) **True** Principle: Managers are individually responsible for whatever occurs in their domain of authority irrespective of the circumstances.

3) **False** Principle: Management control of employees stifles empowerment. Responsible delegation assigns a task to an employee based upon her or his level of *demonstrated ability to perform* (personal empowerment).

4) **False** Principle: "*Feeling* empowered is the Grand Canyon away from *being* empowered."

5) **True** Principle: Direct managers are responsible and accountable for supporting the success of a team under their supervision.

6) **True** Principle: Commitment is *confirmed* when the inevitable difficulty of greatest challenge is successfully overcome.

7) **True** Principle: Managers are 100% accountable for breakdowns just as they are accountable for successes.

8)   **True**   Principle: "The buck stops here!" — Harry S. Truman

The objective of these suggested answers and principles is not only to clearly understand what is meant by the definitions of personal responsibility, accountability, and empowerment on pages 25, 26, and 29, but to create a whole new paradigm of thinking.   Such a paradigm has the power to put an organization in a truly unique class in terms of high employee involvement. The widespread adoption of this organizational mindset is a requirement for becoming a high performance organization illustrated by the diagram on page 11.

Interpersonal Team Skills

One of the reasons for instructing the team to reach consensus is that it is rarely achievable in a one-hour time frame. Thus, the team members resort to what they most commonly do in pressured situations in order to achieve agreement. The result is typically a vote. Voting is an example of *individual expression* in which the majority carries. This is *not* consensus as defined on page 38.

Consensus in a Japanese way of operating is probably not the best way for U.S. Americans to operate. Perhaps, somewhere between the two is optimal. We suggest "collaborative agreement."[2] The definitions of these two terms capture the essence of what we mean:

- Collaborative — to work jointly with others

- Agreement — harmony of opinion or action; mutual understanding.

44

Adopting this approach can result in the efficient use of time while simultaneously maximizing input and team alignment.

Since constructive interpersonal behavior is important for effective team operation, your group might discuss what each of you discovered about your own behavior in that exercise using as a guideline the list of interpersonal team skills described below:

1) **Self-observation** — the examination of our feelings, emotions, and behaviors in relating to others who are different and think differently:
   - dominating a discussion
   - being inwardly (or outwardly) angry
   - cutting others off
   - not being open and receptive to differences
   - defensiveness

2) **Open Communication** — the *experience* of being free to honestly express opinions different from others:
   - allowing complete explanations
   - expressing yourself fully even when there is a reaction
   - encouraging others not to interrupt
   - being concise, brief, and to the point

3) **Suspension of Assumptions** — the willingness to set aside beliefs about others and what they have to say:
   - realize that assumptions are rarely accurate
   - avoid making unsupported charges
   - ask for clarification where assumptions are made

- create dialogue around the issue which is most troubling

4) **Dialogue** — to be totally open to another's point of view in a discussion:
    - listen to our own self-talk
    - attempt to set the self-talk aside
    - "put yourself in another's moccasins"
    - express your point of view in a convincing manner

Finally, each of your team members might discuss how she or he plans to use these insights to behave differently in the future.

A Foundation of Empowerment Exercise

We have suggested that personal responsibility, accountability, and empowerment are the foundation upon which high-involvement is based. Upon closer examination, these concepts are also an inherent part of practically every task or project we do in life. The interrelationship among these three concepts is illustrated in Figure 5. When assigned a project or a task, the detail and inclusiveness of planning is directly proportional to one's "willingness to assume total responsibility," as a predisposed mindset. This mindset determines whether the plan will be well thought out, taking into account unforeseen contingencies, or superficial and subject to unpleasant surprises. The level and quality of performance, as a process, is primarily a measure of one's previously demonstrated ability to perform — *personal empowerment*. Where the requirements of the project or task require greater competence than has been previously demon-

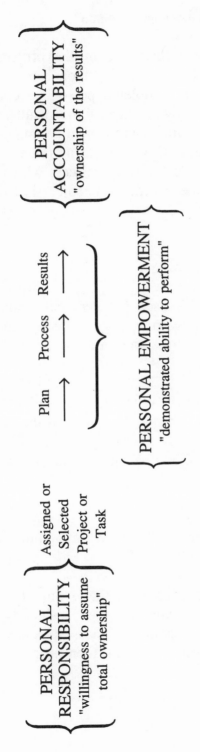

Figure 5. The interrelationship between Personal Responsibility, Accountability, and Empowerment as applied to a project or task.

47

strated, the successful performance of the project or task simultaneously results in expanded personal empowerment. When the project or task is completed, personal accountability simply means "claiming ownership of the results," without reasons and/or excuses. In order to practice empowerment, these three concepts have to be learned as *functional skills*. The following exercise illustrates the process which you will need to apply and practice in order to become skilled at using these concepts.

An Empowerment Exercise

Using the definitions discussed for personal responsibility, accountability, and empowerment, generate applications of each of these concepts to some task or project in your organization.

Personal Responsibility: "What is the opportunity for expanded employee empowerment?" (What is the objective?)

> Learn to mentor self-management to a willing employee.

Personal Empowerment: "What/How am I going to do it?" (What do I need to learn?)

1) First and foremost, confirm that *I* am good at self-management. If I am not, then I should enroll in mentoring/self-management classes and/or have someone mentor me. If I am, then proceed with this exercise.

2) From my experience, determine what I believe to be the three (3) most needed employee's self-management skills:

    i) Personal responsibility and accountability (mindset; cognitive skill).

    ii) Personal planning and/or organization (functional skill).

    iii) Personal execution and focus on task(s) (functional skill).

3) Use an Empowerment Assessment to measure the employee's strengths and weaknesses and follow up with one-on-one facilitation in the areas of weakness.

4) Assign a significant "stretch project" and jointly agree upon a plan which the employee owns.

5) Meet weekly (or as necessary) to assess and mentor the employee's skills of organization, execution, and focus. Also have the employee assess my performance as a mentor.

Personal Accountability: "How do I measure/evaluate what I do?" (How do I assess my learning?)

1) Do a 360° evaluation by my employees and peers regarding my ability to self-manage.

2) Acquire joint agreement between the employee and myself regarding the specific self-management skills required of the employee, *before proceeding*.

3) Hold the employee responsible and accountable for project agreements. Use broken agreements as an opportunity for facilitating a self-management skill. (Is the employee allowed to slide by?)

4) At each weekly discussion, evaluate the employee's performance and progress in the specific areas of planning, organization, execution, and focus; give specific feedback for improvement.

    Evaluate (grade) the employee's skill at the completion of the project. (Did new learning occur?)

5) Have the employee do a mentor's feedback report evaluating the mentor's performance.

6) Based upon pre-established measures, ensure that the project is successful.

Notice that each of the personal accountability measures are directly tied to the personal empowerment actions. The essence of the actions for personal empowerment is summarized by the question, "What new mindset, skills, and competencies must I learn in order to successfully execute this task or project?" In a like manner, the summarized question in personal accountability is: "In what ways could I hold myself and others *unquestionably* accountable for having accomplished this task or project?" This requirement is, by far, the most difficult and challenging to master as a functional skill. The extent to which empowerment will ultimately work depends on the courage of the change agents to practice this skill, *with integrity*.

Use the format below and on the following page to practice this exercise in an area of empowerment that is of interest to you.

Personal Responsibility: "What is an area for improvement or what is an opportunity in empowerment?"

Personal Empowerment: "What am I going to do and/or how am I going to do it?"

1)

2)

3)

4)

5)

Personal Accountability: "How do I measure/evaluate what I do?"

1)

2)

3)

4)

5)

By repeatedly practicing this three-step process for your personally chosen stretch projects, personal responsibility, accountability, and empowerment will become functional skills.

CHAPTER SIX

PERSONAL EMPOWERMENT — A PERSONAL GROWTH PROCESS

Most writings on empowerment rarely, if ever, discuss the relationship between personal empowerment and personal growth; yet, the two are interdependent. The ability for full self-expression, as well as working productively with others, is critically dependent upon how well we have resolved intrapersonal and interpersonal issues. As long as we design our lives to remain in comfort zone situations, such issues relating to our performance rarely surface. However, in high people involvement management systems, interpersonal issues are an integral part of the operation and are rarely avoidable. They invariably surface quickest in the formation of new teams as described in the following examples.

A major R&D organization, implementing empowerment, put into operation several self-directed teams across exempt/non-exempt lines. In the initial stages of operation, most of the non-exempt team members acquiesced to the strong suggestions of exempt employees and managers. Gradually, productivity began to fall below the level before the teams were formed, in spite of the fact that the improvement projections showed an increase of 50% as teams. When breakdown forced a heated team discussion, what surfaced were beliefs and attitudes about inferiority/superiority, elitism/classism, formal education/on-the-job learning, and a

53

general lack of mutual respect among team members. The team spent the next three months resolving these issues while progressively approaching their projected level of productivity.

On a much less intensity level, we are also continually learning life's little lessons through our daily array of interpersonal interactions called "the workshop of life."

The "workshop of life" is *the* most impacting personal growth process in which everyone is engaged — some consciously, but most of us unconsciously. Personal growth is the sum total of our day-to-day experiences that result in our gradual life-long process of knowledge and maturity. We enrolled in this workshop at birth and we will be engaged in it until death.

The experience which results from this life-long process of expanded empowerment is transformation. In simple terms, transformation is the invalidation of conflict-producing, counterproductive, and/or self-limiting beliefs. The essential nature of transformation is that it is irreversible and comprehensive in every aspect of our lives. Since we rarely understand ourselves at the level of our most deeply hidden beliefs, *conflict and/or limited performance are life's feedback signals letting us know we are being driven or limited by one of these subliminal beliefs.* Since we tend to interpret this feedback as something is wrong with someone else or some situation external to us, we generally transform by an almost imperceptible evolutionary process — except when we experience a significant crisis or illness. These experiences tend to involuntarily "slingshot" us into expanded maturity and a more harmonious adjustment to life.

Consider Allen, the manager who after many years began to notice that he continually had difficulties with individuals who did not appear to be working "all the time." Completing a task early and taking a break, or taking time to chat with a co-worker was interpreted by Allen as wasting time or just plain laziness. Naturally, he would intervene with corrective action, which worsened already strained working relationships. Then, in the course of a relationship training, Allen was facilitated in rediscovering a phrase his mother often repeated and which he had obviously adopted, "Idle hands are the devil's workshop." That phrase, coupled with his "Protestant Ethic" upbringing, had become not only a *guiding* principle, but a *driving* principle in his life. He not only applied it to himself, but also unconsciously to others whom he managed. This realization was a breakthrough and totally transformed his ability to give up control. Allen developed a new aspect to his management style — focus on results and productivity and pay less attention to style and details of the process.

The relationship of Allen's personal breakthrough to empowerment was his newly found ability (after overcoming a personal barrier) to continually minimize the necessity for management, and maximize his focus on proactive accountability only to the extent necessary. This ability began to show up not only in the workplace, but also in his personal life.

A less stressful way to become personally empowered, as an ongoing process, begins with the conscious acknowledgement and acceptance that transformation is an inherent part of the human experience. Then, become aware of the myriad of ways to proactively engage the process; both in personal and professional situations. The guiding criterion is that the process or method used is *personally appropriate* and fits you.

The least confrontive means of engaging the process of personal transformation is by reading books and listening to tapes on self-improvement, followed by conversations with people with whom you feel comfortable. In order to more actively engage the process, you might utilize the variety of personal development courses and seminars offered by your organization in both intrapersonal and interpersonal skills. Basic courses in intrapersonal skills typically involve self-responsibility and accountability, stress management, time/life management, and decision-making, whereas those in interpersonal skills involve problem-solving, relationship, communication, and organizational management. More advanced offerings in personal development involve diversity, leadership, creativity, and quantum-thinking. If your organization does not make such courses readily available, then you have a personal responsibility to acquire personal development with your own resources. After all, it is an investment in your future, even though your company may also have an obligation that it is either unable or unwilling to fulfill. In summary, personal empowerment — the process — is synonymous with personal growth.

The CEO of Planedome Industries, Inc. preferred to work alone. He found it difficult to understand his human resource department's increasing demands for empowerment training for management. He had already authorized thousands of dollars for the quality initiative training. Why didn't people just do their jobs? Whatever happened to the good old fashioned work ethic? When the empowerment consultant suggested that he go through a 360° assessment to determine his level of living and modeling empowerment behaviors, he resistantly agreed. When he had an opportunity to discuss challenging feedback in a private session, he began to view his involvement, behaviors, and commitment as viewed by others as central to the success of his company. He also began to view training as an important part of the education process for workers acquiring new knowledge. At the end of the session, he thanked the consultant for relieving a lot of his anxiety around change, high-involvement, and the need for knowledgeable employees.

The Role of Training

As the U.S. becomes more and more dominated by knowledge and service industries, we will *have to* value training as an integral and ongoing part of doing business. Since we tend to be so systems-oriented, we often ignore how vital people-oriented skills and competencies are in terms of productivity and the bottom line. *The* workplace phenomenon driving the need for regular training is the recent transition from the information era to the present knowledge-based era. We are beginning to understand that business competitiveness is based upon realizing that knowledgeable workers are the continuing source of new products. As such, the key is to encourage and support self-motivated personal *and* professional growth.

II. TEAMWORK

"And it is still true, no matter how old you are — when you go out into the world, it is best to hold hands and stick together."

"All I Really Need to Know I Learned in Kindergarten"
Robert Fulghum

CHAPTER SEVEN

TEAM EMPOWERMENT

We believe that the increased popularity of teaming over the past ten years is because teamwork is probably *the* crucial component in successfully implementing and sustaining high employee involvement programs; namely, Quality, Reengineering, ES&H, and of course, Empowerment. The establishment of high performance teams, which require a high level of commitment to the group in preference to one's self, is very challenging to U.S. Americans. The reason is, the most fundamental core value of U.S. Americans is individualism, commonly expressed in terms of personal freedom, personal achievement, and personal reward. However, the necessities and benefits derived from teamwork far outweigh any reluctance we may have about fundamental change required to embrace teaming. Proven benefits resulting from teamwork are: increased productivity, efficiency, quality, commitment, and a more flattened organizational structure.[3]

Although many organizations view Teaming as an initiative comparable to Quality, we tend to view it as *the* major means of implementing high-involvement. This view prevents the process of implementing teams unnecessarily, but as dictated by necessity, efficiency, or opportunity. We must keep in mind that, in the U.S., individual contribution and reward will probably always be important in our way of functioning, based upon our most fundamental core value of individualism.

Therefore, U.S. teams will probably always have a component which stresses individual excellence.

Team Empowerment

In general, a team is a collection of individuals who must rely on group collaboration and support to experience success or achieve their goal. Typically, there are no redundant roles, except in the case of large projects. The central idea behind a team is the assumption that a strong collective approach is ultimately more powerful in consistently producing quality results, while maintaining the team members' well-being, than pitted competition between individuals in the same organization.

Given this definition for a team, we can readily see that the degree of autonomy of operation can vary significantly from "manager directed teams" to "total self-directed teams." This variation of operation is described by five types of teams, shown in Table 1. The central theme in these descriptions is the progressive increase of independent operation corresponding to increasing individual and team empowerment.

Team Empowerment is the capacity of a group of individuals (a team) to operate in an independent manner in proportion to their individual and collective competencies and skills. The greater the demonstrated (or evaluated) competencies and skills, the greater the autonomy. As a team moves through the various designations, corresponding to greater autonomy (Table 1), the relinquishing of management and supervisory control is the key factor to the team's success.

Table 1. Team Designations and Operations as a Function of Individual and Team Competence

Team Designation	Function
1) Manager-Directed	Manager assigns the project and team members, and manages the team process in the traditional manner.
2) Manager-Participant	Manager selects the projects and becomes part of the team. Team functioning is more egalitarian, but manager has the final decision.
3) Manager-Facilitator	Manager and team members are selected by the nature of the project, i.e., cross-functional, quality, customer, etc. Manager is an equal team member, but is acknowledged to bring necessary facilitative skills to the egalitarian team operation.
4) Manager-Coordinator	Manager is not a team member. Team members are selected by the nature of the project. Team operates autonomously within specific guidelines. Manager assures quality, customer satisfaction, team objectives, and where necessary, coaching and mentoring.
5) Self-Directed	Little or no management involvement. Manager may act as a consultant. Team selects projects or tasks, is self-managed, and is held *accountable* for continuing to earn its independent operation. Continuous-learning is a way of life.

63

A basic premise of team empowerment is that the most productive team is realized by the development of each team member through personal empowerment. Therefore, a particularly important element for U.S. teams, in their interdependent operation, is the full expression of individual excellence. However, no team member is ever more important than the team.

Team empowerment also implies that each team member is *simultaneously* 100% individually and 100% collectively responsible and accountable for the results produced by the team, as an operating principle. Therefore, each team member has not only the obligation, but the responsibility, to hold himself or herself accountable for his or her performance, as well as the performance of the other team members. As a team progresses through the various designations in Table 1, team members begin to *experience* this reality to a progressively greater extent, as a working principle.

Manufacturing Technology, Inc. had embarked on its ISO 9000 certification process with fanfare and enthusiasm. The organization was capable of meeting the certification deadline established by its president, but it would require a stretch. The quality assurance coordinator brought technically capable individuals together from different areas of the company to form teams. He made roles and responsibilities clear as he delegated aspects of the certification. He worked to make sure that everyone knew how what they were doing affected other teams in the certification process. As meetings took place over time, some teams began to experience interpersonal conflicts and blamed their lack of progress on inadequate resources and management control to make the changes they needed. The quality assurance coordinator could see that a new kind of mindset was going to be needed. A mindset which emphasized individual and collective ownership for the success of each team as well as the overall process.

He decided to "reestablish" basic assumptions which were taken for granted:

1) Communication of the necessity for the certification.

2) Commitment to the purpose and the goal.

3) Alignment and ownership of the certification.

4) Provision for basic needs and resources.

5) Confirmation that the goal was compelling.

6) Establishment of a team acknowledgement/reward system.

Criteria for Team Efforts

Team empowerment allows a team approach to the achievement of an objective when necessary *and* an individual approach when a team effort is unnecessary or inappropriate. Organizations operating at the far right of Figure 1 (pg 8), such as W.L. Gore and Associates, are dominated by teamwork. Very little, if any, of their activity involving a whole piece of work, is an individual effort. Whereas organizations more to the left of Figure 1 (pg 8) incorporate a balance between individual contribution and teamwork as is necessary.

Team efforts are more appropriate than individual efforts when:

1) No one person has all the information or expertise to accomplish the objective or goal within a given time frame.

2) There is a need, benefit, or value to working across disciplines or divisions.

3) Several or many points of view are necessary to solve difficulties or problems relating to the objective or goal.

4) A group naturally prefers a team-oriented approach *and* productivity and employee well-being are not compromised.

5) There is a necessity (or opportunity) for greater productivity, quality, and competitive advantage through team synergism.

It is important to note that each of these criteria fall into the category of necessity, efficiency, or opportunity (or a combination).

Team Empowerment Leadership

The more empowered a team is in utilizing the combination of individual competencies, the less necessity there is for directed individual leadership; what emerges is *participative leadership*. Leadership takes on a completely different meaning in empowered organizations. If the team members are self-motivated and self-directed, then there is no need to lead in the traditional sense. Leadership may constantly change depending upon what situation the team might be experiencing. Most often, team members are not at the same level of personal empowerment. Those who have developed their full capability inspire others by their performance. Their predisposed motivation is to *be a difference*; that is, leading by example. *Retrospectively*, we may describe their participation as having made an important difference.

Principles of Team Empowerment

1) *The team is principally (if not totally) self-directed.*

   An empowered team assumes maximum responsibility and accountability for planning and implementing their tasks or projects in proportion to their demonstrated ability to perform. As the team's competency and performance increase, their freedom to operate independently proportionately increases to, ideally, complete self-management.

2) *Individual excellence is maximized within an interdependent network.*

   Individual excellence is an integral part of full self-expression and should be encouraged *within* an interdependent network. This principle assumes that the team's performance capacity is in direct proportion to the collective capacity of its individual team members. However, this capacity is *only* realized when no team member is considered more important than the team and they work to create synergy.

3) *Personal responsibility, accountability, and empowerment are maximized.*

   Expanding one's personal responsibility, accountability, and empowerment is a continual process of personal development which serves to maximize one's professional performance. The greater the ownership of these three personal characteristics, the more fully one's capacity to perform is realized (see Figure 5 on pg 47).

4) *The team "Code of Conduct" governs expected team behavior.*

Empowered teams *require* a "Code of Conduct" which applies equally to all team members, irrespective of an individual's ability to perform in an exceptional manner. This "Code" serves to set guidelines of expected behavior for enhancing the synergism of the team's performance.

5) *Trust, cooperation, and participative leadership are valued.*

Fundamental values common to empowered teams include the team members' willingness to foster a context of trust, cooperation, and rotating leadership roles based upon their various competencies. These essential values are key elements of the "Code of Conduct."

For example, a diversity team from the ENSERCH Corporation created the following Code of Conduct:

- **Sensitivity** — We will, as a team, be sensitive to each other by practicing awareness, understanding, patience, and acceptance.

- **Accountability** — We will, as a team and individually, be dependable and responsive, and honor **all** our agreements.

- **Relationship** — We will, as a team, be committed to relationships which are genuine and supportive.

- **Equality** — We will, as a team, interact as equal partners for the overall success of the team, regardless of position or rank within the organization.

- **Communication** — We will, as a team, commit to open, honest communication — actively listening for new ideas and direction.

- **Respect** — We will value the diversity of our team, demonstrating respect by consistently maintaining confidentiality and non-judgmental attitudes.

6) *Mastery of interpersonal skills and competencies is valued.*

When empowered teams are comprised of highly competent individuals, interpersonal dynamics emerge as a limiting factor to team performance. In fact, the extent to which a team can self-facilitate interpersonal compatibility is the extent to which they will ultimately realize their full potential. Mastery of this potential is therefore *the* limiting factor which determines whether a team progresses to the stage of self-directed.

7) *Diversity is valued.*

Diversity is manifested in the myriad of ways teams are put together: examples include multicultural teams (necessary for global competitiveness), cross-functional teams (important to customer service and product development), and self-directed teams (critical to quality improvement). Dimensions of diversity such as race, sex, ethnicity, culture, workstyle, age, etc. play a major role in the efficient operation and ultimate success of empowered teams.

8) *Alignment with and commitment to the team's strategies, objectives, and goals are necessities.*

A team is not a team (empowered or not) until team members are clearly aligned and their commitment to strategies, objectives, and goals is unquestionably established. If any perception of a question exists (even from an "intuitive feeling"), it should be brought up for discussion and resolution. If put off, it will later emerge with greater counterproductive intensity.

When a project, task, or work process has been identified as a team effort and the team members are selected, the implementation process begins. A unique approach to this process is discussed in the following chapter.

CHAPTER EIGHT

IMPLEMENTING TEAM EMPOWERMENT

Implementing team empowerment (or becoming an empowered team), usually begins by responding to three key questions:

1) What areas of responsibility, within a given organizational unit, could a team of individuals perform more productively with the least amount of control or direction?

   These areas may fall into two categories: 1) those responsibilities which the team is already capable of handling and require the least amount of coaching, and 2) those responsibilities which would be "a stretch" and require significant coaching, new learning, and very specific guidelines.

2) What new mindsets and competencies must the team acquire, individually and collectively, in order to perform the new expanded responsibilities at a customer-demanded level of expectation?

3) How could the team members hold themselves unquestionably accountable for having learned the new mindsets, skills, and competencies, *and* for having successfully performed the task or project at the level of customer expectation or beyond?

These requirements are best established *before* the project or task begins and should have definitive metrics (or measurables) involved in the evaluation. The more specific and definable the accountability measures, the more successful the process *and* the project. The more nebulous the accountability measures, the more confusing and less effective the process and the less likely the success of the project.

After responding to these three questions, an area of expanded responsibility for self-direction should be identified. In addition, new learning and accountability measures should also be clearly defined. Based upon the responsibility, the team composition is defined by employees involved in the identified process or selected on the basis of the expertise demanded by the task, project, or work process.

The following example illustrates the application of this sequence of questions for a customer-focused service team.

A Team Empowerment Example

Responsibility: What's the opportunity?

Develop a strategically aligned, customer-focused service team.

Empowerment: How are we going to do it?

1) Create a "Code of Conduct" or "Team Value System."

2) Align our team with the customer's organizational or business unit vision.

3) Add value and/or profitability to the customer we are serving.

4) Evaluate and address the need for continuous team training in order to provide quality service to the customer.

5) Be knowledgeable of the cutting-edge opportunities in alignment with serving the customer.

Accountability: How do we measure/evaluate what we do?

1) Brainstorm session: "What's absolutely necessary to have a customer-focused service team that exceeds customer expectations?" Select the top five and define their meanings. Examples include: trust, commitment, communication, relationship, diversity, etc.

2) Evaluate if our activity is inclusive of our customer's goals (short-term or long-term).

3) Determine (and/or calculate) how our activities increase the efficiency and/or profitability of our customer's operation.

4) Do in-house team training (where necessary) and track progress with well-known diagnostic instruments to measure our progress.

5) Appoint a rotating team member to collect information relative to the up-to-date advances in the areas of interest of the service team's activities. Have a team evaluation of the implementation and/or effectiveness of this continuous-learning process.

The Team Empowerment Process

Having identified a "stretch" project, task, or work process and a "preliminary team," the team empowerment process proceeds by the team responding to the following set of guidelines:

1) **Define the purpose of the team.**

   - Why does the team exist?
   - What is the team's objective or goal?

2) **Define the roles and responsibilities of the team.**

   - Is each team member clear about her or his role?
   - Does each team member know the roles of the other team members?
   - Does the team have all the expertise necessary? If not,
   - Utilize existing organizational expertise and support when lacking among team members.

3) **Define the mode of operation of the team.**

   - Establish a working vocabulary for important terms. (pg 176)
   - Establish a mode of leadership and an accountability system.
   - Discuss team trust, relationship, communication, support, commitment, etc.
   - Establish a team "Code of Conduct" or "Value System."
   - Decide on a team operating designation as defined by Table 1 (pg 63).

4) **Select a manager to coach and set guidelines for the team.**

- Manager and team should agree on guidelines.
- Manager and team should establish accountability in terms of quality, productivity, and team functioning.
- Manager should coach as is necessary.
- Manager should provide the necessary resources for the team to experience success.
- Manager and team are clear on overall team responsibility and accountability, what support the team will receive from the organization, and what specific authority the team has to meet their objective.

5) **Utilize training as an integral part of team empowerment.**

- Take training to understand and use team empowerment.
- Training in technical, organizational, and interpersonal skills must be an ongoing part of the process.
- Integrate "just-in-time" training into the process as required (i.e., interpersonal skills, coaching, holding others accountable, etc.).

6) **Proceed to function with established management accountability checkpoints.**

- Assess team operation and objectives shortly after beginning.
- Assess team operation and objectives at half completion.
- Use crisis as an opportunity for a breakthrough.
- Assess team success at completion.

7) **Evaluate team performance at completion.**

- What worked?
- What did not work?
- What did we learn for future teams?
- What do we need to learn for future teams?
- Establish a new team project (with fewer guidelines) and "Go for it!"

At the successful completion of each task or project, where a "stretch" has been involved, the team acquires a greater capacity to perform independently; ΔE (quantum jump in empowerment).

This capacity is evaluated jointly by the manager (or team leader) and the team as a basis for establishing clearly defined expanded guidelines for future team operation. The "sphere of team competence" (hereafter referred to as the *sphere*) is the measurable or demonstrated ability of the team to perform at or above customer expectation. Thus, Figure 6 shows a continuing process of expanded team empowerment (ΔEs).

The dots represent start and endpoints of a stretch project. The solid line circle represents the process. ΔE ($E_{final\ state}$ - $E_{initial\ state}$) is the increased capability of the team, both individually and collectively. The sphere is represented by the successively larger circles (combination of solid and dotted semicircles). As the *sphere* becomes progressively greater, the more the team assumes responsibility for self-selection of projects and self-management. The ultimate state of team empowerment is total self-direction.

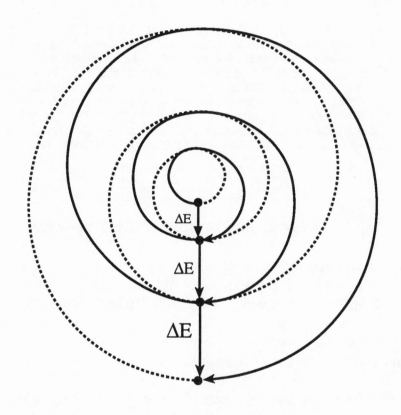

Figure 6. Sphere of Team Competence

"We are going to organize ourselves into teams and each team will have a team leader," announced the product development manager. It sounded good to Maria. "Now maybe we can focus on one thing to completion" she thought. As their first project began, it became increasingly clear that the team leader needed specific guidelines beyond "ready, set, go!" What sounded like a good idea became chaotic and business as usual. When the manager realized how errant the process had become, he sought out a facilitator to help him and the team get back on track.

Although tedious at first, the team settled into a clearly defined process of implementing team empowerment that produced measurably better results. It soon became clear that teaming was going to be a challenging process of learning new responsibilities and skills. The most challenging to Maria's team were interpersonal and administrative skills as well as being directly responsible for meeting customers' expectations. At times her team wondered whether it was what they *really* wanted. What kept them going, in spite of their doubts, was the realization that their team performance was the best security they could have during a period of downsizing.

Stepwise Process of Implementing Team Empowerment

In this sequential process of *initiating* team empowerment, the manager and team leader may be the same person. In addition, we recommend that the titles used be adapted to your organization's language. The important elements of this sequence, we have learned from our experience, are clarity and appropriateness of functions.

1) Manager assigns a specific project with a due date to a team, typically 5 to 15 individuals (appointed or self-selected). Team leader determines the level of individual and group responsibility and accountability and makes sure each member understands his or her individual and team role. Team leader is also responsible for making sure all group members have the necessary skills.

Management Intervention One (MI-1)

Manager consults with team leader about individual and group responsibility and accountability. If needed, an Empowerment Assessment can be conducted to assess levels of individual and team empowerment.

2) Team creates a plan for successfully accomplishing the assigned project by proposing increased authority and greater opportunity for decision making.

Management Intervention Two (MI-2)

Manager reviews proposal in light of individual and team levels of empowerment. Manager and team jointly decide what level of decision-making authority will be allowed and clearly agree upon the expanded boundaries and responsibilities of the team. Manager and team jointly agree on how to proceed.

3) Team leader (or manager) works closely with team members in the early stages of the project, providing necessary mentoring, coaching, and feedback. Both the team leader and manager should be careful not to undermine newly granted authority. In some cases, management should allow teams to be unsuccessful rather than interfering. This can provide a critical learning experience and should be viewed as an investment in future success.

Management Intervention Three (MI-3)

At one-fourth completion, manager evaluates the team's progress, focusing on results, not process. Manager emphasizes customer satisfaction and needs and the necessity for meeting jointly established deadlines.

4) Team has regular meetings (at least once a week) to
    determine both individual and team progress. The team
    process depends on the willingness of individuals to
    hold each other accountable without the necessity of
    management intervention.

Management Intervention Four (MI-4)

*The team leader (or manager) should facilitate the
team in an evaluation of each other's performance.
Manager should coach highly empowered team
members (including the team leader) on how to coach
others. Manager coaches marginally performing team
members to assume expanded responsibility.*

5) The manager evaluates progress at the half-way point.
    If there is marginal performance, the manager
    proactively (non-punitively) holds the team accountable
    for results and provides an opportunity for the team to
    resolve difficulties without management intervention.
    If this is unsuccessful, the manager must facilitate the
    team, incorporating whatever degree of empowerment
    possible.

Management Intervention Five (MI-5)

*Manager provides leadership by showing the team how
the crisis is an opportunity for growth. Manager uses
breakdowns to teach empowerment principles and, if
needed, facilitates the learning of interpersonal skills.
If necessary, the manager may want to consider
additional training or using an in-house or outside
human resource consultant.*

6) Once the difficulty has been overcome, the team
    proceeds with the project, striving for greater quality,
    service, and productivity by incorporating lessons

learned from the breakdown. Team members hold a brainstorming session on how they can improve the final product or service and *exceed* customer expectations.

Management Intervention Six (MI-6)

Manager offers support and asks the team what resources they require in order to successfully complete the project. Manager should be prepared to meet their requests. This helps establish a new context for manager-employee relationships based on empowerment and trust.

7) As the project nears completion, the team identifies how they have met and/or exceeded originally established objectives through personal and team empowerment.

Management Intervention Seven (MI-7)

Manager acknowledges successes of the team and appropriately rewards the members. This is also an opportune time to review the empowerment vocabulary so that it becomes integrated into the organizational culture.

8) Team successfully completes the project.

Management Intervention Eight (MI-8)

Manager calls a meeting with all team members. This is an opportunity to openly discuss the successes and drawbacks of the entire process. Topics could include new interpersonal skills that were developed as well as targeting future training needs. Manager and team discuss how to improve the process in the future. If appropriate, utilize written team evaluations.

Team Evaluation

At the completion of your team task or project, you might use the two following evaluation exercises in order to maximize your learning and establish team objectives for the next task or project.

In the first exercise, each team member individually responds to each Yes or No question below, based upon his or her experience of the team's performance. At the completion, Yes and No responses for each question are compared and discussed by the team. Where there is disagreement, the discussion should involve where breakdown occurred and how it might be avoided in the future.

TEAM EVALUATION

		YES	NO

1) Did you decide each person's role and responsibilities based upon what she or he was most skilled at doing or learning? ___ ___

2) Were you clear about your role and responsibilities in the task or project *before* you began the implementation process? ___ ___

3) Did your team *avoid* repetition of process and ensure quality because *each team member* had a high degree of quality awareness and performance? ___ ___

4) Did your team utilize each team member in the *most effective manner*, by not having two or more people working on a one-person task or compensating for a team member's lack of performance? ___ ___

5) Did your team prepare, *as best it could* during the planning phase, for implementing the project? ___ ___

6) Did you (personally) experience minimal interpersonal conflict or irritation in performing your responsibilities interdependently with your team members? ___ ___

YES NO

7) Based upon your team's performance, did you work as effectively *as possible* as an empowered team (based upon your initial team competence)? — —

8) Did your team's leadership style encourage maximum self-direction and team trust? — —

Exceptional success for the team in this evaluation exercise is when team members unanimously respond Yes to each of the eight (8) questions above.

To use the second exercise below, each team member evaluates himself or herself in the "Self" column according to his or her team performance. Select the most prominent characteristics by not checking more than 15 of the 29 available. Then, "write in" the characteristic he or she believes would improve most his or her team performance in the (1) blank space.

Each team member then evaluates every other team member in terms of his or her perceived team performance, again selecting the most prominent characteristics (not more than 15). It is not necessary to have proof or an explanation for selecting a characteristic for another team member; use your intuition or perceptions as feedback of your experience. "Write in" the characteristic you believe would most benefit each team member in his or her team performance in the blank space.

TEAM PARTICIPATION INTERACTION
(How Do Others Perceive Us)

Personality Characteristics	Self					
1.						
2. trusting						
3. leadership						
4. reserved						
5. commitment						
6. creative						
7. arrogant						
8. valuing others						
9. sensitive						
10. supportive						
11. demanding						
12. understanding						
13. persistent						
14. intelligent						
15. open communication						
16. aggressive						
17. accepting of others						
18. domineering						
19. impatient						
20. unmovable						
21. sense of humor						
22. risk-taker						
23. cooperative						
24. emotional						
25. responsible						
26. knowledgeable						
27. intuitive						
28. flexible						
29. interdependent						

At the completion of the team "Self and Others" evaluation, create a process for each team member to receive feedback from every other team member for all 29 characteristics. For example, for a five person team, an individual team member may receive any number from 0 to 4 for any of the characteristics listed. She or he may also receive several recommendations ("write in" characteristics) for functioning more effectively as a team member from number (1).

The frequency of a specific characteristic provides valuable feedback as to how a team member is perceived by the group. Each of these can be compared with how an individual perceives herself or himself from the "Self" column. This comparison is sometimes surprising to a team member and leads to new awareness and learning from the feedback. Finally, the characteristics most frequently selected by team members for an individual can be compared with the important team-building characteristics shown below:

Important Team-Building Characteristics

2)	Trusting	12)	Understanding
3)	Leadership	15)	Open Communication
5)	Commitment	17)	Accepting of Others
6)	Creative	23)	Cooperative
8)	Valuing Others	25)	Responsible
9)	Sensitive	28)	Flexible
10)	Supportive	29)	Interdependent

The *lack* of acknowledgement by the group of any of these characteristics provides a specific area of new learning or competence for each team member to master.

CHAPTER NINE

BEYOND TEAM EMPOWERMENT — SYNERGISM

In the advanced stages of empowered team functioning, a new opportunity arises. The opportunity is to function at an even higher level of performance which goes beyond the sum of the team members' talents and abilities. This level of performance is called Synergism. Team Synergism is similar to that described by Peter Senge in his book, "The Fifth Discipline."[4] This level of team performance requires *Personal Mastery, Team Creativity*, and *Individual and Team Learning*.

Personal Mastery

The first requirement of a synergistic team is that the individual team members achieve a relatively high level of personal mastery. Personal mastery is the combination of self-actualization and professional competency to perform at a level which exceeds the expectations of others. It is characteristic of individuals who "live their lives with passion and pursue their bliss," in the words of Joseph Campbell.[5] Life is a continual pursuit of excellence. In addition, the practice of introspective self-awareness is an ongoing process.

This individual makes a distinction between knowledge and wisdom. Knowledge is what one knows, whereas wisdom is one's *way of being*. Wisdom is what drives the humane application of knowledge in service to others. For example, an individual who has come to the *experiential* realization that all human beings are inherently equal, would probably embrace diversity "because it's the morally right thing to do," rather than having to have a "fool-proof" business necessity.

Personal mastery is most commonly played out by the team's "Code of Conduct" (or value system). Most teams include in their team values: trust, communication, relationship, diversity, and alignment. Regardless of the specific Code of Conduct, the practical question is, "How is a team member facilitated when she or he inevitably violates a team value?" Personal mastery focuses on the complete acceptance of the person while simultaneously requiring each team member's commitment to the team values in terms of ethics and behaviors. If an individual continually violates the team's values, it becomes necessary to evaluate the appropriateness of the person to be part of the team. In this case, the evaluation is not based upon professional competency, but upon the degree of deviation of the individual's behavior from the team's Code of Conduct. For synergistic teams, team integrity is as important (if not more) than individual competency. Individual competency is assumed to be a given.

Team Creativity

The second requirement of a synergistic team is the realization that team creativity supersedes individual creativity. That is, the focused alignment of several individuals creates within the team a meta-level of creativity. This is commonly done by using a four-stage creative brainstorming process projected five to ten years into the future. The four stages are four segmented time periods (15-20 minutes each) in which the group progressively brainstorms ideas further and further from the present reality. Then, they creatively connect these futuristic ideas back to the presently existing mode of operation. The sequence of steps (ideas or products) provide the "stretch" goals for the team sourced from the team's synergism. The premise of the process is that the ideas generated by the team are at a higher level of creativity (and challenge) than would be possible for individuals alone.

When the challenge was first introduced to the group, Allen was positive he had the best solution and worked to convince everyone to accept it. He felt himself growing resentful when someone suggested they all "look beyond the obvious" and go for a more creative approach. Everyone began to get excited about trying "dream state" creativity. Allen thought about running away from the whole thing but decided that even though their methods were getting "farther out," this was the place to be to keep learning. At least he knew the old traditional creative methods were no longer as effective in his present fast-paced environment.

After several weeks of practice, the group was astounded by their abilities to collectively create new ideas having several dimensions of application. It appeared, at times, that they were able to create a connected network of their individual creative ideas. The result was extraordinary creativity leading to the next generation service or product.

Individual and Team Learning

The third requirement is an adopted mindset of continual individual and team-learning (or collaborative learning), *as a way of life*. The greatest barrier to team learning is the (individual and group) resistance to overcoming self-imposed limitations rather than the ability to learn. Such limitations are so subtle that they are not consciously recognized by individuals and groups. This is why groups, at this level of performance, benefit measurably from regular external facilitation. The key to knowing whether such barriers exist is by the direct observation of results or performance measures.

Individual and team-learning occurs where the following interpersonal elements are present in the way the team functions:

1) Self-observation

2) Open communication

3) Suspension of assumptions

4) Dialogue

5) Consensus decision-making

Self-observation is the willingness to focus one's attention inwardly to one's own thoughts and feelings. If we view the outside environment (i.e., team functioning) as the source of a never-ending sequence of events (stimuli) which may or may not challenge the way we think, then those events which are in conflict with our beliefs instantaneously provoke feelings of a threat (fear). Self-observation means that we have developed an ability to connect our feelings to our triggered belief, as the first step. And secondly, we have learned to honestly examine the validity of our triggered belief with respect to the external event. This process provides the opportunity for change and personal growth.

For example, self-directed team members are constantly in the process of balancing maximum self-direction and the need for a manager-coach during their growth process. The greater the extent to which their ego-drive for control can be set aside to honestly evaluate their proven competency as a team, the more productively the process of total self-direction can be accomplished. The same is true for the manager-coach in dealing with her ego-drive in giving up control to allow the team to set "stretch goals" which are realistic. The source of this element of synergistic team functioning is self-observation.

Mark had never participated with a group where he was not "in control." He had come from an academic background where "results are everything" and he was used to being ultimately responsible for getting them. In his heart, he felt no one was as dedicated or committed as he was. No one on the team appeared to put in the time or effort in continuous-learning that he did. He eventually concluded that, in the final analysis, he could only depend on himself. The people around him consistently made mistakes and resisted feedback for doing things better.

o o o

As Maryanne experienced her teammate Mark, she wished she knew why he always appeared to be dissatisfied with the group's performance. He had a lot to contribute, but people were growing tired of his incessant attention to mistakes and continuous improvement. It was hard to understand why someone like Mark who expected perfection would want to work with others. Maryanne decided to invite him to lunch to learn more about his point of view and work toward a new level of team performance. She was confident that with open communication she could understand his point of view and begin to establish a win/win situation.

o o o

What they discovered is that conflicts are rarely, if ever, one-sided. Their righteous self-talk only served to stifle the team's growth. Maryanne's courage in creating the meeting with Mark was the breakthrough that came from self-observation of her own thoughts and feelings. The meeting with Mark provided the opportunity for the examination of the validity of their self-talk. Success, in their discussion, would depend on the second step of the process, open communication.

Open communication begins with the establishment of an environment where feelings, emotions, and a wide divergence of ideas can be expressed with little or no objection. Divergent ideas are simply viewed as part of the spectrum of discussion topics necessary to secure team alignment. It is important to recognize the fact that open communication is an ongoing process. As team members experience greater and greater team cohesiveness, barriers between and among themselves must, of necessity, be dealt with.

For example, a sales team which had been together for three years began to experience a more difficult time reaching decisions which had previously been routine. One of the team members shared that she "experienced a sense of heaviness" in their meetings and felt that one of the team members was not being truthful with the team. When the accused team member gained sufficient courage, he finally admitted to the group that he no longer wanted to be in sales and eventually left the group.

The point is this, in order to operate at peak performance as a team, there must be no hidden agendas. When necessary, the team members must sometimes draw out someone who is stifled by his or her own reluctance to tell the truth. The eventual result of not doing so will be some form of subtle (or not so subtle) sabotage as a prelude to leaving the team.

Suspension of assumptions is the willingness to acknowledge that we unconsciously judge most everything we hear and set aside our judgements. This ability connects to self-observation in that by simply observing our mind's conversation about the matter at hand, we are freed to more openly "observe" what someone else is proposing. This literally requires us to view the world through another's eyes or "walk in someone else's moccasins" (the original American Native saying). As an exercise, think of someone you disagreed with in a recent exchange of ideas. Project yourself into that person's mind. Imagine their childhood, their history, family associations, education, and recent sequence of experiences. If you had that individual's history and present life situation, would you probably think like him or her? This sense of empathy can also be acquired by carefully observing someone's behavior in order to create an environment where their freedom of expression is maximized. By seeing the world through someone else's eyes, our judgements and assumptions are simultaneously suspended.

Dialogue is a state of team functioning where the flow, dynamics, and integration of ideas create synergism. In order for dialogue to occur, all of the previous elements of team-learning must be present. For example, in a recent team discussion of how we might "reengineer"[6] the process for producing seminar workbooks, we all came to the conclusion that our discussion was about improving the existing process. This group realization provided the opportunity for us to see that we were avoiding the necessity of our own fundamental change for reengineering to occur, either in terms of our competence and/or new technological integration. This realization allowed the breakthrough to shift from *discussion*, to *dialogue* around such questions as: "How few hands need to touch the final seminar workbook?", "What new competencies, skills, and technology would be necessary for one person to do the entire process?", "What is lost in efficiency and new learning by having only one person handle the entire process?", and "How do we optimally reengineer the process?" The result of this dialogue went from ten pairs of hands in the process to three.

Consensus decision-making is the process of creating committed alignment. It is the culmination of the elements discussed above. It may occur in a variety of ways, depending upon the situation. For example, when an expert is part of a team, it is not uncommon to defer to that individual's recommendation after sufficient team discussion and dialogue. On the other hand, most team decisions are made by a consensus process which takes into account a wide spectrum of viewpoints. This does not necessarily mean the final decision is an "average" of all points of view and certainly not a vote, but is one which is simultaneously "progressive" *and* "integrates the spectrum of differences expressed by the group." It ultimately integrates everyone's point of view into the final decision. This is necessary for commitment.

The use of "systems thinking" is an excellent example of a new team competency for a synergistic team. The following example illustrates the integration of this process using the Foundation of Empowerment principles discussed on page 47.

Personal Responsibility: "What new area of professional mastery could our team learn to significantly enhance our synergistic performance?" ("What's the opportunity?")

Master "Systems-Thinking" — for individual and team problem solving.

Personal Empowerment: "What new mindset, skills, and competencies must we learn in order to successfully learn this new technique?" ("What/How are we going to do it?")

1) Read Peter Senge's book, "The Fifth Discipline."

2) Each team member writes a one-page summary of designated chapters read and shares them with the team for questions, clarifications, and feedback.

3) Apply the "systems-thinking" approach to a specific team problem or opportunity.

4) Practice, practice, and practice until "systems-thinking" is mastered as a tool.

Personal Accountability: "In what ways could we hold ourselves *unquestionably* accountable for having learned (mastered) this technique?"   ("How do we measure/evaluate what we committed to?")

1) Read two chapters per week.   Total of 21 chapters, completion of book in 10 weeks.

2) Allow for question and answer period from team members to ensure everyone's understanding of each chapter summary.   Have team members grade each other.

3) Use the expanded systems picture to locate the activity of greatest leverage (locate the "trim tab") for the problem or opportunity chosen.

4) Mastery occurs when the application of this skill solves the problem.   See Figure 7.

Systems-Thinking Example

Figure 7 illustrates a systems approach to dealing with an organization's drop in sales/market share.

Top Circle: Short-term (low-cost) obvious solution involves upgrading the marketing process and/or materials coupled with an expanded and more forceful effort in sales.

Result: In some cases this approach does bring about a short-term increase in sales/market share.   Eventually, sales drop again because the problem is more fundamental.

Business Unit Problem: Drop in sales/marketshare

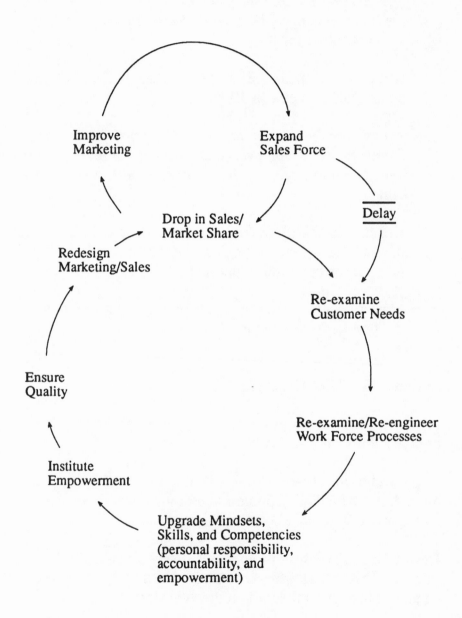

Figure 7. Systems-Thinking Example

Lower Circle: The systems approach, which involves the identification of the various dimensions of the business operation which impact sales, is much more inclusive and fundamental.

Delay: The "delay" indicates the time frame necessary to attempt the short term solution (top circle) until the realization occurs that it will not solve the problem. At this point a shift to the lower circle occurs.

In systems-thinking, the "point of leverage" (or the trim tab) is an activity in the lower circle which has the "greatest impact" in solving the problem. In this example, it is "upgrading people skills." If this activity is effectively pursued, it affects all the other activities in the lower circle.

III. ORGANIZATIONAL SUPPORT SYSTEM

*"A support system provides
nurturing, resources, commitment, and
an expectation of performance."*

The Authors

CHAPTER TEN

THE ORGANIZATIONAL SUPPORT SYSTEM

Besides competent employees, an Organizational Support System is *the* most crucial component in successfully implementing an empowerment initiative. An Organizational Support System consists of the following three major components:

1) Organizational Leadership

2) Management Commitment

3) Empowerment Infrastructure

The discussion of this part (Part III) of the text follows the flow diagram for the comprehensive implementation of empowerment shown on pages 166-168.

Organizational Leadership

The organizational leadership plays a pivotal role in instituting cultural transformation. Their process begins with acquiring the information and knowledge necessary to become committed to the empowerment initiative. An inherent part of becoming committed involves the personal process of creating an internally-sourced empowerment vision, the acquisition of passion for the vision, and the inner knowing that when the inevitable difficulties and setbacks occur, she or he will prevail. In instituting empowerment, adversity, setbacks, and continual uncertainty are certainties. The only question is "How do we prevail in spite of these obstacles?"

For example, a common situation leadership experiences is employee resistance to greater accountability corresponding to greater delegated authority. Such situations provide a convenient excuse for leadership (and management) to return to hierarchical operation. The committed leader convinces managers and employees that hierarchy is not only unacceptable, but an unworkable alternative in today's competitive world. High-involvement, delegation, and accountability are all necessities for effectively operating in today's business environment and are non-negotiable.

In a similar manner, it is not uncommon for management to strongly resist, not only their ("apparent") loss of control, but their necessity to master new interpersonal management and team skills. The energy and persistence necessary to overcome these objections can be enormous. Again, aggressive, committed leadership must make it clear that the change process is non-negotiable. Management anxiety and resistance are understandable, but will not prevent the necessity for empowerment.

When Gene began the empowerment initiative, he loved the idea. Finally, there was a way to get greater employee buy-in to business success. After one year, when he still heard complaints about managers and quality was no better, he called his Vice Presidents together and wanted an explanation. "We've all been through the empowerment training" one VP volunteered. "I guess we're not really sure what you want us to do." Gene sat stunned. He slowly and carefully chose his words. "Let me be clear. You are responsible and accountable for ensuring that you push decision-making and problem-solving to the lowest levels of the organization. People must be prepared for their new level of responsibility. This will be a part of your

> performance review and tied to your bonus. What support do you need to be successful? We are not going back if we are going to stay competitive."
>
> The reality that Gene was experiencing is that empowerment is a long-term process and shows the least results in the first stage, which may be one or two years. He was also learning that the process will not succeed by a leadership directive to "go forth and empower your people." Leadership must play an active role in promoting the empowerment initiative and establishing a permanent support system.

The leadership must clearly communicate to the organization the rationale for the new vision and the value to the organization. This must be *continually* done in a sufficiently inviting and persuasive manner that it is accepted and embraced through self-enrollment by a critical segment of the work force. An essential part of this communication process involves the clear articulation of the organization's Guiding Principles. For example, the Guiding Principles for the Texas Instruments Empowerment Initiative are shown below.

GUIDING PRINCIPLES FOR AN EMPOWERED
TEAM-BASED ORGANIZATION
Defense Systems and Electronics Group (DSEG)

Principle 1:   We will create business strategies that provide opportunities for sustained competitive advantage and individual growth. Achieved through:

- Customer focus
- Continuous improvement (coupled with breakthrough improvement)
- People involvement

Principle 2:   Sustained breakthrough performance improvements will be achieved through work design/business process engineering advancements coupled with technological advancements.

Principle 3:   We will design our business processes to include only value-added activities that are required to meet customer expectations.

Principle 4:   Every Tler is responsible and accountable for achieving business objectives. Critical dimensions for ownership:

- Capability at the point of execution
- Information at the point of execution
- Decision-making at the point of execution
- Recognition, rewards, and advancement tied to the effectiveness of both the decisions and the execution.

Principle 5:   We will foster a commitment to DSEG's objectives, values, and beliefs by creating an environment which aligns them with the individual Tler's objectives, values, and beliefs.

Principle 6:   Continuous-learning will form DSEG's foundation, enabling increased responsiveness, flexibility, and innovation.

Principle 7:   We will reward and recognize Tlers based on both achieving organizational (DSEG/ Business Unit) expectations and demonstrating desired individual behaviors. Desired behaviors include:

- Empowering leadership

- Innovation and creativity
- Collaboration/teamwork
- Honesty and integrity
- Continuous-learning

Principle 8:   Our fundamental working relationship will be one of partnership where we share knowledge, information, responsibility, risk and success. Partnering factors:

- Necessary capabilities
- Common objectives
- Interdependency
- Mutual trust
- Diverse perspectives

Principle 9:   We will value diversity.

Principle 10:   We will live by these guiding principles without exception.

In summary, it is leadership's role to *live* the vision and *model* the principles.

Management Commitment

The role of management is to "make it happen." This segment of the work force is literally "caught in the middle" of the change process. Most of these individuals have devoted years to being "good citizens" and contributing to the success of the organization and should be acknowledged for their contribution. However, with the incorporation of empowerment, they are now faced with a dramatic change in job security, roles and responsibilities, and status. In order to secure their commitment, it is vital that they be facilitated through this transition by education, training, and a shift in mindset in terms of their new roles.

The natural consequence of high employee involvement is a conscious or unconscious process of flattening the hierarchy. The more competently employees perform independently, the less necessity for managing. The less necessity for managing, the less meaningful is the boss-employee relationship. What emerges is a collegial relationship and the merging of *multiple* levels of organization into *fewer* levels.

In many cases, employees are already sufficiently competent to assume expanded responsibilities for which they have not been granted authority. Such cases are the most traumatic for managers who have not continued to improve their own competencies and skills. Thus, job security becomes their major concern when conscious reduction of the hierarchy is a major implementation practice. This situation is quite different from those where highly competent, contributing managers and employees are "downsized." We believe these situations are caused primarily by poor leadership planning in forecasting and anticipating the future.

Another factor faced by management is the significant change in roles and responsibilities. The new roles involve transition from:

1) Manager to facilitator

2) Controller to delegator of authority

3) Organizer to coordinator

4) Supervisor to coach

These changes require both a transformation in mindset *and* the mastery of new competencies and skills. Perhaps the more difficult of these is the transformation in mindset.

A manager's mindset can be affected in two major ways. One is the loss in prestige which comes from no longer being a "manager" or a "supervisor" in the traditional status sense. Second, is the loss of power, authority, and control which were traditionally synonymous with these titles. The truth is these roles represent hard work and achievement, and should be acknowledged as such.

However, in empowered organizations, power, authority, and control are more synonymous with high performance than they are with position or title. Therefore, the transformation in mindset necessary is to adopt a way of thinking which views a valuable, influential employee as one who performs competently with the least amount of oversight or direction. It is not unusual that most managers (and employees) will have to go through some form of the five step "Death and Dying" process discussed by Elisabeth Kübler-Ross:[7]

1) Denial

2) Reaction

3) Bargaining

4) Guilt

5) Acceptance

Facilitating an individual, a team, or an organization through this process is an essential part of any cultural transformation. The essential elements in facilitating this process are:

1) Surfacing employees' beliefs which are the source of their fear of change,

2) Discussing and invalidating those beliefs which are self-limiting or have no basis in reality, and

3) Convincing employees that they are significantly more capable and resilient to change than they realize.

If this process is bypassed by overemphasizing techniques, methodologies, and measurements, the change initiative will surely be unsuccessful. For example, numerous organizations have attempted quality, empowerment, and reengineering initiatives with almost total emphasis on "how to do it." Inevitably, the initiative stalls and is subsequently abandoned. The underestimated, and possibly most difficult, part of the change process is the shift in mindset from "I do what I'm told" to "I take the initiative to learn new competencies and skills in order to remain a value-added employee."

Managers who successfully navigate the five step Kübler-Ross process, by a skilled internal or external facilitator, become an organization's most valued resource in the empowerment transition. First, we doubt that empowerment can successfully take hold on any permanent basis without significant management commitment. Second, managers and supervisors bring years of practical experience and know-how about how the system works and how things get done which can make the successful implementation of empowerment infinitely easier. Again, the key is to have managers (and supervisors) accept and commit to their new roles and responsibilities. The changing roles and responsibilities of managers will be discussed in detail in Chapter 12.

Empowerment Infrastructure

Simply stated, without an empowerment infrastructure to oversee and support the process, the empowerment initiative will be unsuccessful. The following sequence of actions discussed below correspond to the flow diagram beginning on page 166. Establishing an infrastructure begins with an oversight group, such as a task team or steering team. This group is usually representative of the entire organizational structure, particularly those segments crucial to the success of the initiative. It is usually coordinated by someone from the leadership ranks who reports directly to the CEO and/or president. An additional support senior executive, who may or may not be part of the team, is an empowerment champion. This is an individual who is passionately committed to empowerment. This individual must be able to devote 50% or more of her or his compensated time to this activity over several years. It is also necessary for members of the task team to have compensated time as they begin to play key roles in the implementation process throughout the organization. For example, most organizations have full-time empowerment facilitators to assist business units and teams with the implementation process. These are individuals who have gone through extensive training and have been taught critical facilitation skills.

After the task team goes through its own process of education and commitment, implementation usually begins with fact finding, analysis, and some form of an organizational empowerment assessment. This assessment should provide an evaluation of individuals, teams, leadership, and the overall organization in terms of their readiness to initiate the empowerment process. The assessment should also serve as a baseline measurement (relative to future measurements) as well as identifying specific areas of weakness. For example, it is not unusual when beginning an empowerment initiative to discover that employees are more competent to perform independently than they have been allowed to. Management and leadership interventions are usually the first areas for addressing this situation in terms of training, education, and commitment. An initial assessment also reveals that holding self and others accountable is a common weakness in most organizations. Thus, preparatory education and training are essential to prevent initial accountability difficulties relating to breakdown in expectations.

At this point, the task team begins the process of formulating an empowerment plan. An essential part of this process is a planning session where the various functions of the empowerment infrastructure are clearly established. The culmination of the planning session, several weeks later, is a detailed empowerment plan. In practice, most organizations begin training and implementation processes *before* they seriously consider a support infrastructure. Therefore, the *logical* sequence I have described is rarely followed and is not a necessity. What is necessary is the realization that, at some point in the process, instituting an empowerment infrastructure will be necessary for success.

Now that we have briefly discussed the three major components of the Organizational Support System, let us explore the function of each of these in greater detail in the following chapters.

CHAPTER ELEVEN

THE ROLE OF LEADERSHIP

We define leadership as the impetus which drives an organization in the achievement of its vision. Leadership is the driving force which transforms vision into reality. If the vision is challenging and ambitious, then the corresponding level of leadership commitment will have to be great. Committing to empowerment, or any of the transformational changes, such as quality, diversity, etc., can be difficult. The reason is, we cannot really know the extent of our commitment until we encounter the inevitable difficulty of greatest challenge, and successfully overcome it. Commitment is discovered midstream when we are most challenged by the process.

For example, when we discover, by experience, the investment of time and energy required to have employees perform in a self-accountable manner, it might appear easier to go back to the hierarchical/management way of operating. It is only after we learn that initiation of empowerment to any significant extent is a door we have entered which has subsequently disappeared, do we come to the conclusion that the only question is *how* do we make it work. In a like manner, the reality of the loss of management control of information, power, and process can be equally traumatic.

"This sounds a lot like the passengers flying the plane to me," Eric thought. "Everyone's empowered and doing whatever they want. . .great." As time went on, Eric began to experience that the clearer he was about what he expected, the more able he was to put the right people on the right job and let them go.

He learned to provide 3 crucial elements:

1) Clearly defined responsibility and accountability to the team.

2) Availability to support people when needed.

3) Delegation of authority at the level of ability to perform.

The level of commitment required of leadership is greater than that required of management and the work force, in the sense that leadership has the power to stop or sustain the process. In most cases, commitment solely from a business perspective will probably not be sufficient to successfully implement empowerment. The reason is, the high degree of personal and organizational transformation required will naturally generate a high level of resistance and probably unconscious sabotage. Particularly in organizations which are relatively healthy and profitable and do not *have* to change in the short term. For example, the most common tactic used by some employees who resist change is simply to ignore it. They willingly go through any training and planning required and then proceed to ignore implementation. The thought which commonly runs through this employee's mind is "I'll know they are serious if they are still singing the same song a year from now and someone steps in to hold me accountable." Therefore, leadership will ultimately have to also be committed from an internal source which translates into passion. The internal source which most often inspires leadership commitment, beyond business motivations, is a shared vision of the future. This passionate commitment must be sustained over several (or many) years before substantive change begins to occur.

Therefore, the role of leadership in proactive organizations, attempting to *anticipate* change, is particularly challenging and simultaneously exciting! We outline, in sequence, the process of committing to and leading an empowerment initiative. Again, this discussion follows the sequence outlined on pages 166-168.

Education and Awareness

One of the major roles of leadership is to be knowledgeable of major changes occurring in business operation. Aside from the competitive advantages inherent in high employment involvement, are the four necessities we discussed earlier — *quality, customization, speed,* and *service* — which require this mode of operation to simply survive. A critical part of the education process is to discover how these four necessities relate to your particular organization or business operation. For example, a central theme in the implementation of quality is having more employee contact with the customer. In order to operate effectively in this capacity, employees must learn skills formerly reserved for managers and sales people. They must learn how to ask relevant questions and, most of all, learn how to listen to what a customer *needs*, so that these needs can be anticipated. The knowledge and training necessary to perform in this expanded capacity are essential ingredients of an empowered employee.

In addition to the practical connections of empowerment to the business operation, leadership must be exposed to a comprehensive understanding of an empowerment program (pg 166). That is, realization of the possible challenges, consequences, and opportunities — both within the framework of business necessities and the growing desire of employee self-expression. As organizations streamline for high performance, they simultaneously retain those employees who require the least amount of supervision and/or direction. It would be counterproductive and outdated to retain a high degree of hierarchy and structure — and ultimately unworkable with such employees.

The final step in the process of committing to empowerment is exposure to an *in-depth experience* of the challenges of empowerment, such as sharing power, giving up control, rewarding performance (rather than position), reducing hierarchy (management), and transforming fundamental personal beliefs. An effective seminar (or workshop) should include these elements, in addition to education. After commitment is established, there should be ongoing education and training involving implementation strategies and skills consistent with the new philosophy. Empowerment, by its very nature, is a continuous-learning process for *everyone*.

Having this in-depth exposure to empowerment provides the basis for the initial stage of an organizational (leadership) commitment. The secondary commitment to such an initiative occurs when a comprehensive plan has been developed with the corresponding financial support necessary. As stated earlier, the "moment of truth" commitment occurs when an organization's greatest unique issue(s) of resistance surfaces and the leadership, management, and employees successfully resolve the inevitable issue(s) and proceed to constructive implementation.

Leadership Practices and Procedures

The fundamental rule for credible leadership is "*live* the vision and *model* the values." Living the vision involves adopting a mindset that the vision is already a reality. It literally exists,

114

at present, within the minds of leadership. Their everyday experience of the workplace, in turn, creates this expectation in others, and ultimately the reality. Leaders essentially project themselves into the vision and literally pull the organization into that future reality.

This process takes form by the establishment of both personal and business objectives and goals. It also involves setting the direction of business units consistent with the organization's vision and goals by written and verbal communications, being the head cheerleader, and modeling high-involvement behavior.

In its attempt to communicate the importance of teamwork to the organization, Texas Instruments reorganized its traditional leadership structure into a leadership team structure. The new structure is a "circle" of eight critical business functions with a core leadership team of three executives. The core team is titled the "Office of the Chief Executive." This reorganization provides the opportunity for broad input and consensus, participative decision making, and cross-functional teaming at the executive level.

Modeling the values is being a living example of the expectations of others in terms of behavior. It does not mean being a martyr or an assumed "Sainted One." It means leaders will violate the values, on occasion, just as other employees. Particularly where there are strong pressures to "achieve business objectives and goals, no matter what you have to do." This is usually the "moment of truth" for a leader. The situation(s) where values, morals, and ethics have to be reconciled with "business necessities." In indeterminate situations, i.e., downsizing, environmental concerns, societal impact, etc. decisions are made by judgement rather than solely on the basis of information and analysis. Judgement is based upon an organization's vision, mission, principles, and values, and ultimately upon an individual's morals and ethics.

In order to have an organization which operates and behaves in an ethical manner consistent with the organization's values, it is leadership's role to institutionalize education and training as an integral part of organizational functioning and an *expectation* of all employees. This emphasis must be maintained until education and training are viewed as an integral part of the job rather than a distraction from "real work." Upgrading leadership qualities and skills training must be an ongoing process, as a necessity, for high-involvement organizations. This process also involves the utilization of information technology, networking, and organization-wide information sharing, i.e., TV monitors, E-mail, videotapes, interactive multimedia learning, etc.

Finally, it is leadership's responsibility to continually mentor and coach new leadership. A central objective might be the planned selection of a diverse group of high potential employees to be mentored for future leadership. In other words, leadership is responsible for overseeing, evolving, and when necessary, transforming the culture. This process is ideally accomplished through the conscious mentoring of the type of leadership required for the future.

The New Leadership — The Future is Now

In the present knowledge-based era, success is in direct proportion to employee competence and well-being. This reality has caused organizations to become more people-focused in terms of employee quality of life. Employee quality of life is the *experience* of being fully valued, included, and provided the opportunity for full self-expression in terms of one's capabilities and talents. As leading organizations have become more people-focused, a new dimension of leadership has simultaneously emerged. That dimension involves doing what is ethically, morally, and socially right, even when it is not a business imperative. For example, visionary CEOs who realize that diversity is inevitable, need not be forced to aggressively implement diversity because of "provable business necessities." They *lead* from a spiritually-sourced motivation of commitment to total employee inclusion *in addition to* responsibly managing the health of the business. The two are not incompatible! This description of the "new leadership" has similarities to that described by Peter Block[8].

Similarly, those business leaders who embrace systems-thinking and view themselves as an integral part of their community, also assume a moral obligation to its overall welfare. They do not view this obligation as solely philanthropic, but a natural part of the connectedness of the human condition. We define the latter examples as spiritually sourced leadership. Spiritual leadership is the impetus which drives an individual or a group to act in a way which is in the best interest of the business, the consumer, the environment, and any other components of the system which may be affected. This action includes both short-term and long-term impacts.

Spiritually-sourced leadership is also reflected in organizations which are committed to preserving the environment and protecting consumers without the necessity for exhaustive scientific proof of the dangers of their products. In the long, and sometimes short, run all of these non-hard line business issues do result in very dire consequences for businesses, consumers, and the environment.

In 1991, the business leaders of Dallas, Texas initiated a challenging process for more effectively including ethnic minorities into the mainstream of Dallas business. The result was the creation of the Dallas Together Covenant for Workplace Diversity and Minority Business Opportunity. The Covenant, a *first-of-its-kind program*, is designed to improve economic opportunities for ethnic minorities. The Covenant has been signed by more than 200 businesses in the Dallas area. It involves publicly stating and subsequently reporting, on an annual basis, minority business commitment in terms of: 1) The dollar amount of purchases from minority-owned businesses, 2) The ethnic minority percentages of new hires, and 3) The ethnic minority percentage of professional / management / board positions newly filled.

Given the interconnected nature of the world today and the accelerated rate of events, the necessity for spiritually-sourced leadership is now. And it will become an absolute requirement for 21st Century leadership.

Leadership Implementation Strategies

The following items are a checklist of those empowerment implementation strategies that leadership is ultimately responsible and accountable for ensuring. Although some of these may overlap with the activities of the empowerment champion and the empowerment task force, leadership has the ultimate responsibility to ensure their effective implementation.

1) Create an empowerment vision.

2) Establish empowerment objectives and goals.

3) Establish management expectations and accountability.

4) Provide empowerment education and training for the entire organization.

5) Establish an empowerment task force.

6) Select an empowerment champion.

7) Confirm and support a comprehensive empowerment plan.

8) Ensure ongoing executive leadership education and training in empowerment.

9) Reduce unnecessary levels of management as a function of expanded organizational empowerment.

10) Ensure an empowerment infrastructure.

11) Encourage and provide employees with greater information, knowledge, power, and rewards.

12) Acknowledge and reward empowerment successes.

13) Create a climate for a learning organization.

The process of getting these items done involves the commitment and cooperation of management. We now turn our attention to the radically changing roles and responsibilities necessary to manage empowerment.

CHAPTER TWELVE

MANAGING EMPOWERMENT

As we have stated previously, the role of management is to "make it happen." Making it happen requires commitment. Commitment does not occur as a result of a directive from upper management or leadership. It occurs through education, training, and the opportunity for managers to confront and invalidate the fears they experience as a result of the change process. A crucial part of the education process is the realization that high employee involvement is a competitive necessity for which we have no choice. Once this reality has set in, we can proceed to begin the implementation process.

Managing the implementation of empowerment requires defining and learning new skills, namely:

1) Responsible delegation

2) Coaching

3) Interpersonal relationship and communication

4) Fundamental changes in traditional management functions to facilitation

5) Holding others accountable

Although this list is not exhaustive, it does include the crucial elements that managers are immediately faced with when implementing empowerment. These will be discussed in turn below.

Delegation and Coaching

Two basic concepts which relate to the effective management of empowerment are responsible delegation and coaching. Delegation is the act of granting authority to an individual or team of individuals to perform a task or an assignment for which he, she, or they will be held accountable for the results produced. Responsible delegation is delegating within an individual's or team's capability or slightly beyond.

In the dictionary, the word empower is defined as "delegation with authority." When applied to the *practice* of managing empowerment, confusion arises when a task is delegated to someone who does not have the demonstrated personal capability to accomplish the assignment. Can you truly *empower* someone to do something they are not capable of? The answer is, of course, "no." For this reason, we have chosen to make a clear distinction between personal empowerment and delegation, as it applies to the workplace.

Personal empowerment is an internally-derived capability to perform while delegation is the act of being granted authority to demonstrate that capability. Therefore, a manager cannot personally empower an employee or a co-worker by simply granting authority to perform a task. Within the framework of these distinctions, responsible delegation with authority is an operational necessity for an empowered organization.

The reason this distinction is so vital to understand is because the corresponding expectation involved in responsible delegation is accountability — of both managers and co-workers. Accountability is the willingness to answer for the results produced from an assignment, for which you were given authority. When a task is delegated, it is either within or beyond the capability of the person given the task. This is where managerial judgment and maturity become crucial. When an assignment is clearly within one's capability, success consistently follows, although little or no growth occurs in terms of expanded personal empowerment. Managerial maturity is necessary to know oneself well enough to distinguish situations where one's personal beliefs and attitudes might influence the underutilization of personnel from those involving individuals who are clearly unwilling to grow.

As the deadline grew closer for certification review, Joe knew it was going to be close. He had brought people through this process nine times before in various companies where he worked and he knew how to do it. "Meeting the deadline" was Joe's excuse for going into a "command and control" mode to make it happen.

In his review, he was criticized by subordinates for a lack of coaching and his unavailability. "Who has time?" Joe thought, but he knew that wasn't the issue. Just because he had done it nine times before didn't mean it was done the best, most efficient way. He decided to reexamine his process and bring subordinates into the decision making about time schedules up front. "Mostly, I don't trust these people. That's why I don't delegate," he confided to a facilitator. "But it's getting too complicated to do it alone. It's so hard to spend time to get to 'know your people' when all I think is needed is 'Get the job done!' I'm still working on really seeing that people are our most important resource. I have to spend time developing their capabilities or we'll be running in place."

When an assignment is delegated which is beyond the demonstrated capability of an employee or co-worker, coaching is an *inseparable* part of that assignment. A manager or supervisor is obliged to conscientiously assist the empowered growth of that employee *in addition* to ensuring the successful accomplishment of the task. Within the framework of these distinctions, responsible delegation of authority is an operational necessity for an empowered organization.

Coaching is an interactive process, either in pairs or as a team, of facilitating the enhancement of an individual's ability to perform by successfully accomplishing a challenging, previously unachieved task. The result of coaching is the acquisition of new skills, knowledge, and/or an expanded mindset of self-competence. Coaching is fun, yet difficult at times, because it requires the development of interpersonal skills. To know and to tell someone *how* to do something is not difficult. To influence them to risk beyond their comfort zone to acquire expanded capability requires trust. Trust usually results from the process of establishing in-depth interpersonal relationship and communication. A manager is responsible for initiating the interpersonal interaction and openness that leads to the mutual level of trust required.

These issues naturally arise as an integral part of the teaming process. Particularly, where a great deal of self-direction is desired. They are even further exacerbated where teams are cross-functional and/or diverse. Teams must set aside the time and commitment necessary to resolve whatever unique issues they identify in order to effectively serve internal and external customers. This process involves a combination of overcoming (releasing) mutual stereotypical beliefs and attitudes and ethnocentric values, and laying the foundation for a team (or organizational value system) based upon mutual trust, respect, and equality. Such a foundation establishes the basis for the most effective utilization of empowerment as a management style.

Changing Roles and Responsibilities of Managers

The emerging role of managing (particularly middle-managers) in the future has been described by Vogt and Murrell,[9] based upon historical precedent. Our view of these functions, based upon empowerment as described in this text, are summarized in the following discussion.

1) **Evaluating** *where* we are as a team, unit, or division, and *what* it is we need to be doing to increase productivity, quality, profit, and the growth and well-being of employees — Evaluation usually implies a comparison of a present status with a previously established goal or sequence of accomplishments leading to an established goal. If neither of these exists, then such an evaluation may lead to the realization that the team, unit, or organization is not totally clear as to the specifics of what is to be accomplished. "Hazy goals produce hazy results." When an evaluation indicates that established goals are not being accomplished, it raises the question of what should be done differently *and* how do people have to change for these different procedures to really matter. When an evaluation indicates the successful accomplishment of or excelling an established goal, a team, unit, or an organization is in the enviable position of being content or setting higher standards for themselves and possibly the market. In all three situations, the question raised is what do we do about our present situation?

For example, if the real estate market is "soft"; that is, houses are not selling in normal quantities and/or prices are falling, what should we do as an independent office? During difficult times, an organization discovers who is truly committed, and to what extent, to the organization's success. It is typically easy to be involved during good times, but the test usually comes when times are tough. Therefore, what to do may begin with re-assessing individual commitment and making whatever mutually appropriate adjustments are necessary. It also involves going back to basics in redefining such questions as "What specifically do we do or sell?," "Who specifically is our customer/client?," "Are we serving them best of anyone competing?," and "What do we need to be doing differently and innovatively to meet the present challenge?" When questions such as these start to become clarified, it naturally leads to *how* do we change our situation toward achieving success?

2) **Planning** how we go about achieving increased productivity, quality, profit, and the growth and well-being of employees — After answering the back-to-basics questions above and re-assessing the ranks for commitment, the next management *coordinating* responsibility is establishing interdependently, *what you are going for.* What is the goal that begins to define, retrospectively, the stepwise plan for success. Based upon the elements defined above in planning, both systems improvement *and* people development will most often be required. According to the empowerment philosophy, the more employees embrace personal empowerment, the more receptive they are to procedures which ensure increased productivity and quality — and profit naturally follows. It is vital that the team, unit, or organization is intimately involved in the plan so that their ownership of the process is unquestionably established.

For example, if the plan is to significantly increase the quality of a product or service, the team, unit, or organization will have to accept training as an *integral part* of the process, rather than an annoyance that takes them away from the real process. It is vital that they come to realize that training provides the framework for understanding what they are attempting to change. Training is not only a change in the process, but a transformation in their fundamental way of thinking about performing a task. Therefore, a vital component in planning is establishing the value, "Training is important to achieving quality."

3) **Organizing** how to coordinate the total unit's human, financial, and physical resources in such a manner that individual excellence can be achieved within an interdependent team and organizational setting — Even though this is a management responsibility, and she or he will be held accountable, it is important that the team, unit, or organization be involved in this process. The empowered manager's preoccupation is, "How do we organize our activities in such a way that everyone's talent is maximized?' And as a corollary, "How do we ensure the opportunity for expanded personal empowerment and the elimination of personal and professional barriers?"

For example, an empowered manager may organize her unit's tasks in such a manner that she sets the parameters, limitations, and to some extent the organizationally-imposed guidelines, and then requests the unit to establish the procedure for most effectively accomplishing the objective. It is vital in implementing this management style that employees have as much responsibility as possible; *with accountability.* This point is perhaps best summarized by a command attributed to General George Patton, "It's amazing how creative your people will become, if you tell them where to be at what time, and don't tell them how to get there."

4) **Decision-making** that *most effectively* addresses difficulties, problems, or new challenges encountered with the major focus for solutions on those directly involved — Decision-making that involves processes and/or procedures is relatively straightforward and is usually best done by those directly involved. In a like manner, decisions involving policy and explicit procedure typically have straightforward guidelines. However, one of the most difficult responsibilities of managing is making decisions involving people and more specifically, decisions resulting from their performance evaluations. This is a responsibility which requires managerial mastery, not only in making a decision, but carrying it out in the most professional and compassionate manner, particularly where difficult. The basic rule is, "You cannot effectively manage in others what you have not mastered about yourself." Holding others accountable for their performance is, by far, the most difficult characteristic which is necessary for the systematic incorporation of empowerment. The determining characteristic of successful companies in the 1990s will be flexible decision-making based upon a shared strategic vision. This means delegating decision-making powers to middle and line managers, with the simultaneous elimination of unnecessary management layers which stifle self-directed operation. A basic rule of human nature is that commitment to and ownership of a decision is synonymous with participation in the process. For example, many of the decisions involving improved quality customer service results from the direct interaction of line managers and workers with the

customer, without the necessity of upper management's involvement.

5) **Motivating** employees to achieve their maximum potential in an activity for which they are personally skilled and interested, confident of management's support, encouragement, and modeling — This will be a more critical function in a market where organizations will be requiring greater productivity from fewer employees. Rather than giving orders, managers will have to become skilled at motivating, advising, and facilitating. The benefits that come from the successful encouragement of employees to function at their maximum potential will be realized continuously with every project. High performing employees add more to the "bottom line" of an organization's profit than any other single factor. Empowered, and therefore motivated, employees operate continuously in this manner.

6) **Developing** the personal and professional growth of self and employees as an integral part of the empowerment process — The key here is to have employees realize that personal growth drives expanded empowerment and that professional development allows expanded creative expression of their newly acquired skills. Since quality is a market-driven necessity, new creative products and services are required to remain competitive. Development occurs, most effectively, where managers encourage training, interactive mentoring, and professional growth opportunities. In addition, they create an environment where development is not only valued, but is expected and correspondingly rewarded. This is another area where empowered managers lead by example.

7) **Leading** by being a *living example* of the expectations of employees and therefore credibly inspiring exceptional individual and team performance — Leadership is a progressively participative process as a team, unit, or organization becomes more empowered. Therefore, leadership involves making certain that everyone understands and is committed to the established objectives and/or goals, and continually providing the spark that drives the team, unit, or organization to success.

Guidelines for Facilitating the Empowerment of an Employee or a Co-Worker

1) *Clearly explain and describe personal empowerment.*

   Begin with a clear explanation of personal empowerment and a description of an empowered employee. Explain the relationship between personal responsibility, accountability, and empowerment.

   An empowered employee is an individual who has the skills and the capability to solve expected and unexpected problems that arise from an assigned task, with the least amount of guidance and supervision. When guidance and supervision are necessary, they involve new learning in capability, and should not have to be a repeated lesson; although reinforcement may be necessary.

2) *Clearly explain and describe the job (or task) responsibilities and expectations.*

   Provide a clearly explained (and written, where necessary) description of the job (or task) responsibilities

130

and expectations of an employee until he or she clearly understands what the job (or task) entails and what is expected.

3) *Clearly present alternative resolutions to unmet responsibilities and expectations.*

Where necessary or appropriate, clearly explain or write what the recommendations will be if the job (or task) responsibilities and expectations are not met within a given time frame.

4) *Allow ample opportunity to make a decision.*

Allow the employee ample opportunity to decide if he or she is willing to assume the assigned task, given the requirements you have outlined, fully confident he or she has your support and aware that his or her success is the same as your success.

5) *Secure employee ownership of the job (or task).*

Provide an opportunity for employee input and feedback relative to the job (or task) responsibilities, expectations, and evaluation measures, *before* proceeding, such that he or she claims personal ownership of the assignment.

Do not proceed to initiate a project unless there is a clear and/or reasonable level of ownership by the employee.

6) *Determine an appropriate job (or task) which facilitates employee development.*

It is the manager's responsibility to assign a job or task that is within or slightly exceeds the capability of the employee. (This requires managerial mastery, which is an ongoing process.)

131

7) *Establish specific time frames and provide honest feedback.*

As the employee proceeds to accomplish the project, establish specific time frames for progress reports, feedback, mentorship, and evaluation.

Discuss candidly whether the progress, quality, or the performance is meeting expectations established at the beginning of the project.

8) *Encourage employee personal and/or professional development.*

Recommend (or in necessary cases, strongly recommend) that the employee take personal and/or professional training in order to perform at the level of the assigned task.

Where resistance to personal and/or professional development is experienced, explain to the employee the relationship between expanded empowerment to perform and self-limitations, the professional benefits to be derived, and the practical value of personal growth in his or her everyday life.

9) *Where quality of performance does not meet responsibilities and expectations, act as specified in three (3).*

Where the employee refuses to professionally develop to meet the expectations of the assigned task, the manager has one of two options:

  a) Assign tasks which are only within the capability of the employee to perform in an empowered way.

b) Where appropriate, indicate that in the long run, their present capability to perform may not be sufficient for retention in that position. Therefore, transfer, reassignment, etc. may be necessary.

10) *Ultimately, develop a cooperative commitment to personal and organizational empowerment.*

The essence of operating in an empowered manner is that the choice to personally and/or professionally develop to meet job expectations is always with the employee, interdependently with a *committed* managerial and organizational support system.

Summary

Empowerment, as a way of managing, occurs as:

- Holding others accountable while simultaneously being responsible.

- Assuming employees can think and do for themselves, and allowing the struggles and mistakes that employees have to go through to *realize* they possess expanded capability.

- Treating employees as fully capable and able, and an unwillingness to accept them as disempowered and victimized. This must be done with understanding and compassion.

- Coaching, but not taking away the personal responsibility of an employee.

- Mentoring the personal and professional development of employees.

- Ultimately, being an example of that which is required of employees. Employees are measurably more impacted by what a manager does, rather than what a manager says.

Now that we have established two of three major components of an Organizational Support System, we will now discuss the component which propels and sustains the process over time — the empowerment infrastructure.

CHAPTER THIRTEEN

THE EMPOWERMENT INFRASTRUCTURE

The empowerment infrastructure is the support system which ensures the successful implementation of empowerment. It consists of the internal structure, strategies, and processes necessary to sustain the initiative after an empowerment plan has been approved by leadership. The process of creating an infrastructure also involves the identification of key individuals and the roles they play in implementation. The following discussion involves elements of the second phase implementation shown on page 167.

Infrastructure Task Teams

Creating an empowerment infrastructure usually begins by defining essential structures, guidelines, and functions to be performed by task teams. The work of the task teams should be an integrated part of other related initiatives, such as Teamwork, Quality, Reengineering, Environment, Safety & Health (ES&H), etc. Particularly, where the intent is to achieve a high performance organization. The responsibilities of the various task teams are discussed below:

1) **Empowerment Business Impact** — The establishment of:

   i) Sound business reasons for empowerment.

135

ii) The relationship of empowerment to Quality, Teamwork, Reengineering, Environment, Safety & Health (ES&H), and other related initiatives.

iii) The relationship of empowerment to the organization's vision, mission, values, objectives, and strategic plan.

2) **Empowerment Leadership** — The establishment of:

i) An empowerment vision statement.

ii) Principles of empowerment.

iii) A set of clearly defined empowerment objectives (and timetables) which follows from the vision.

iv) Approval and support of an empowerment plan.

3) **Empowerment Organizational Structure and Roles** — The establishment of:

i) An organizational network for *making empowerment happen* primarily using key positions of the existing organizational structure and human resources.

ii) Key individuals who oversee the coaching and implementation of empowerment, i.e., trainers, coordinators, coaches, strategists, consultants, etc.

iii) The roles and responsibilities of these key individuals.

4) **Guidelines for Organizational Levels** — The establishment of specific responsibilities and behaviors expected of:

    i)   Senior Leadership

    ii) Upper Management

    iii) Middle Management

    iv) First-Line Management/Supervisors

    v) The Broad-Based Work Force

5) **Empowerment Communications Network** — The establishment of:

    i) A comprehensive *network* for the publication and dissemination of all information relating to the empowerment initiative.

    ii) A system and vehicles (publications, speeches, seminars, etc.) for the continual communication of the organization's commitment to empowerment until it is achieved.

6) **Empowerment Accountability** — The establishment of:

    i) What management and employees should be accountable for in the area of empowerment.

    ii) How they will be held accountable through evaluations, measurements, metrics, etc.

iii) What consequences there should be, if any, if mutually agreed upon objectives are not achieved.

7) **Empowerment Plan** — The establishment of a comprehensive plan for achieving empowerment which is confirmed by senior leadership if one has not been established at the completion of the first phase.

The responsibilities of the infrastructure task teams are usually initiated as a one or two-day working session. The participants include members of the empowerment task force as well as key managers and employees crucial to the implementation and success of the empowerment initiative.

A subgroup of these participants (and any other important managers or employees) is selected to summarize the work of the task teams and create a comprehensive empowerment plan including goals, timetables, and human and financial resources necessary for success. This plan is submitted to senior leadership for confirmation and implementation. At this point, the infrastructure task teams are disbanded and the plan is overseen for implementation by the empowerment task force.

Designing a High-Involvement Organization

In order to perform the responsibilities of the various task teams, it is necessary for the participants to become knowledgeable about high-involvement practices. Although an in-depth understanding can be acquired from a selected bibliography on page 175, particularly reference 10, the major components are summarized in the following discussion.

A high-involvement organization is one in which employee empowerment is central to its total operation. Individually

and collectively, employees are primarily responsible and accountable for self-management, quality, continuous quality improvement, and controlling the production of a "whole aspect" of the goods, products, or services.

High-involvement is consistent with some of the most cherished American values, such as *personal freedom, individualism, equality, human rights, competition, innovation,* and *entrepreneurship.* Making high-involvement work most effectively will require the balancing of personal freedom and individualism with *diversity, teamwork, obligation to others,* and *loyalty* to organization, society, and country; for global organizations, it may require an overriding commitment to the overall welfare of the world community.

1) **Is High-Involvement the Right Choice?**

Transition from the Information paradigm to the present Knowledge-based paradigm unquestionably confirms that a highly competent and continuously learning work force is an absolute necessity for competing in a global economy. High-involvement is best suited for organizations which provide goods, products, and services which require complex and continually changing processes. Examples include organizations which are involved in high technology, information systems, science and technology, engineering, electronics, consumer products, etc. It is also required for work forces that are highly skilled and required to make continuous decisions regarding internal processes and customers, such as banking, retail, consulting, hospitality, travel, education, healthcare, etc.

The extent of high-involvement is directly proportional to the extent the work force has demonstrated, by performance or potential, the ability to meet or exceed customer expectations using self-management. High-involvement is a necessity for organizations that expect or require organization-wide innovation, individual and/or group focused quality, fast response to problems and customer needs, continuous quality improvement, and a loyal, stable work force.

2) Creating A High-Involvement Structure

In general, high-involvement flourishes in flattened, decentralized structures. Hierarchical, control-oriented structures tend to discourage, if not totally prohibit, high-involvement. One of the major objectives of a high-involvement system is to increase the *span of control*; that is, progressively increase the number of employees reporting to a manager or supervisor. For empowered organizations this number may be as low as 10 or as high as 100 or greater. This is accomplished by the extensive establishment of teams, both temporary and permanent.

Key elements which influence the effectiveness of high-involvement flattened structures are:[10]

- *Information* regarding the total operation of the organization;

- *Knowledge* of one's job and the organizational operation as a necessity for competent decision-making;

- *Power* to carry out independent *and* interdependent decisions; and

- *Rewards* which are tied to business success and performance, and are consistent with an employee's value system.

The organizational structure is like the basic architecture within which the work force functions and is typically represented by an organizational chart. High-involvement is fostered when the organization is centered around customers, products, services, or a combination of these, rather than being structured by function, which inevitably forces hierarchy, since all functions merge at the top.

For large organizations, this is accomplished by the establishment of several or many small autonomous business units, i.e., SBUs, which produce a particular product or serve a particular group of customers. Where integration of small business units is a key factor, there may be the need for cross-functional work teams.

It is emphasized that the transition from management-orientation to high-involvement orientation should be gradual and progressively proactive. The rate should be determined by the extent of individual, team, and organizational empowerment along the continuum on Figure 1 (pg 8).

3) **Work Design**

Work design in high-involvement organizations centers around the extensive expansion of two basic concepts: *individual job enrichment* and *work teams*.

Both of these concepts involve greater employee information, knowledge, power, and rewards. They also involve greater employee *horizontal* and *vertical job expansion* and control. Horizontal job expansion refers to a greater responsibility for the number of steps in producing a "whole product or service." Vertical job expansion refers to greater responsibility for decision-making regarding the work process of a whole product or service.

Individual job enrichment means to delegate to an *individual* a "whole piece of meaningful work" and to hold her or him accountable for the pre-established expectations. Meaningful work means that the individual totally utilizes her or his valued abilities and skills, which in turn has a clearly definable value-added impact. Individual job enrichment is an ideal situation (when possible) for an employee who is "individually-oriented" in a high-involvement organization. A great portion of this employee's work design can be arranged in this manner (i.e. telecommuting). *It is important that such an individual requires an exceptional attitude regarding personal responsibility, accountability, and empowerment, and is self-managed in terms of performance expectations.*

An individual who is given permission to operate in this manner should constantly be in contact with customers and management to know if he or she is meeting expectations and adding value to the organization's products or services. Examples of employees who may work best in this manner are artists and designers who create brochures and marketing concepts and materials as well as individuals involved in research and development.

Work teams are also designed to have a group be responsible for a whole piece of meaningful work. Team sizes vary as a function of necessity for skills. Ideal team sizes are 4-10 members, although workable teams can be as high as 20 members. Team members must be (or become) social beings who are receptive to interpersonal growth. A major advantage of a team approach is that it reduces the need for management and places control in the hands of those closest to the work that requires improvement and/or change. A whole piece of meaningful work for a team is where the total process involves a clear input and output, transformational process, i.e., something produced that was of a distinctly different quality from that inputted. For example, in an automobile assembly line, a team may be responsible for installing the entire electronics system or a marketing firm, responding to a customer's expectation, comes up with a successful creative sales slogan.

Team members require two major types of skills (or training) — technical and interpersonal. Without these capabilities, in addition to the four elements discussed above — information, knowledge, power, and rewards — a team will not operate effectively. *Therefore, it is clear that an initial investment must be made in training and managerial coaching for work teams to achieve expected levels of performance.*

High-involvement teams vary measurably according to the amount of autonomy they have. Teams with maximum freedom are sometimes referred to as self-directed or self-managed teams. Again, the basic rule is that a team is autonomous to the extent of its "demonstrated or potential ability to perform" (refer to pg 63).

Management-oriented teams usually have a coordinating manager to serve as a coach who intervenes when the team is not functioning according to expectations. In spite of this mode of operation, these teams usually have team leaders within the framework of participative leadership.

The major rewards for both individual job enrichment and work teams are internal, such as job satisfaction, job control, freedom, creativity, personal quality control, etc. Very little in the way of additional financial rewards are associated with either of these concepts of expanded job involvement, except in both situations, individuals and teams *are* rewarded for exceptional performance.

As more products and services become complex and there is a necessity for shorter production times, there is also a greater need for work teams, even in cases where a single individual could perform the task alone. In fact, individual projects are becoming increasingly rare.

It is necessary that both the philosophy and practice of the organizational leadership are consistent with both of these high-involvement approaches to work. This objective can be accomplished by the establishment of senior management teams. These teams bring together senior managers in different cross-functional areas to plan more effective customer-focused strategies or to *oversee* the work of one or more teams which were previously supervised by middle managers.

4) Organizational Improvement Interventions

High-involvement organizations benefit measurably from improvement teams and task forces, particularly in their initial stages. As work teams become more empowered, there is less need for permanent improvement teams and task forces.

Audits and assessments, to evaluate team and organizational performance, are essential tools for benchmarking and continuous quality improvement. An Empowerment Assessment is a particularly powerful tool for regular, periodic evaluation of the extent to which individual and organizational empowerment exist in an organization.

5) High-Involvement Management Practices and Procedures

- First, managers should continually seek ways to share information, knowledge, power, and rewards with employees.

- Routinely distribute all non-confidential information concerning a business unit's operation with all employees within that business unit. The more everyone is informed, the better she or he knows the big picture and makes informed decisions regarding her or his work and others.

- Hold regular meetings with employees to constantly remind them of the organization's vision, mission, goals, and values. Managers should *live* the vision and *model* the values.

- Coach employees with the ultimate intent of delegating greater responsibility and/or decision-making authority.

- As employees acquire greater information about the organization's operation and knowledge of their jobs, there should be a sequential process of delegating self management of vacation time, performance reviews, scheduling, office coordination, budgeting, etc.

- Actively encourage technical and personal skills training as an integral part of the job. Managers should be the modeled example.

- Managers aspiring for advancement or greater responsibility should develop leadership qualities and skills in addition to management skills.

- Extensively include employees in all appropriate decision-making processes in a given business unit (participative decision-making). As empowerment is gradually established, allow total decision-making to be the authority of work teams and/or empowered employees.

- Provide feedback and praise for outstanding performance when earned and deserved. These are valued by high-involvement employees.

- Establish a unit-wide evaluation instrument where all employees can evaluate each other bi-annually in terms of interpersonal and professional performance.

- Encourage career planning for all employees and provide the opportunities for the experiences they require for their career plan.

- Establish direct links between employees, and customers and clients.

6) Recognition And Reward System

The most adaptable pay system for high-involvement organizations is a *performance-based pay system.* In this system an employee is paid for her or his value-added knowledge, competence, and skills. This system is radically different from the job-based pay system characteristic of traditional hierarchical organizations. Performance-based pay focuses on the value added to an organization's goods, products, or services rather than on position or job title. Thus, it has the potential for creating career paths where there is no necessity for "upward advancement."

Therefore, as an employee develops multiple skills, based on a solid knowledge base, she or he becomes more valuable to the organization. This individual is also invited to participate in a variety of work teams.

A performance-based system requires a high degree of self-responsibility, self-accountability, and self-management. It therefore encourages the learning of personal skills that go beyond technical competencies.

Although it was mentioned earlier that the primary incentive for high-involvement is not monetary, in some cases these employees may earn more pay than their immediate managers or supervisors.

Performance-based pay systems require substantial investment in training. A severe drawback is that there is no assurance an employee will remain with an organization after substantial investment of time, energy, and money have been made into their development. In spite of this drawback, there appears to be little choice in the investment in their development.

Instituting a performance-based pay system involves:

- Identifying the tasks to be accomplished.

- Identifying the knowledge, competencies, and skills necessary to perform those tasks.

- Ascertaining the extent to which an employee matches the requirements above or has the potential to achieve them.

- Increasing compensation as an employee performs her or his responsibilities at a high quality level with little or no supervision or guidance.

- A continuing increase in compensation as an employee acquires more knowledge, competencies, and skills which directly result in increased organizational revenues or cost savings.

Designing A High-Involvement System — An Exercise

In the course of facilitating an Organizational Support seminar for a major U.S. corporation, one of the tasks was to design a High-Involvement System. The preparation for this project involved a combination of reading (bibliography, pg 175) and practical experiences of utilizing people more effectively. The premise is that, given the opportunity and the expectation of self-motivated performance, most employees would respond positively. The seminar was designed to generate guidelines and behaviors in the three major areas influencing organizational operation — *structure, management practices, and work design.*

1) Organizational Restructuring — "What are some effective means of reducing our hierarchical organizational structure?"

   - Design a planned level reduction process based on an end state of an empowered organization.

   - Organize functions about the customer through cross-functional teams.

   - Foster greater personal and team empowerment (through education, training, and transformation) — reducing the need for management.

   - Value and reward teamwork where managers become team members.

   - Focus more decision-making at the employee level — thereby reducing the need for management.

   - Establish communication systems and networks between key individuals and teams throughout the organization (particularly involving critical customers or markets).

- Focus on disseminating information regarding the "big picture" to all employees.

- Implement technology which gives employees greater access to critical information and opportunities to perform expanded job responsibilities.

2) Management Practices — "What are some management practices which *require* high-involvement?"

- The establishment and follow-through of employee accountability where performance measures have been previously established.

- Responsible delegation, within clearly defined guidelines, with a total relinquishing of control.

- The unquestionable establishment of education and training as a value and also a required performance review criteria.

- The establishment of a mindset that employees are *expected* to be self-motivated, self-managed, competent, and learning continuously as conditions for employment.

- Incorporate consensus decision-making in group projects.

- Form cross-functional teams to perform whole and integrated work projects.

- Increase employee exposure to and direct interaction with customers; ensure decision-making authority consistent with job responsibilities.

- Implement 360 degree performance evaluations of leadership and management.

3) Work Design — "How can our work be redesigned to achieve greater high-involvement?"

- Delegate "stretch" projects with clear accountabilities and facilitated coaching.

- Reexamine all present work processes for possible redesign or reengineering.

- Consciously shift from a management mindset to a delegator/facilitator mindset.

- Require staff to be responsible for a "whole piece of work" (a customer product or service) in a coordinated team capacity — with little or no management intervention.

- Design ways for individual contributors to be internal consultants to empowered teams.

- Create a work experience progression plan which brings employees through critical positions, decision-making, and skills acquisition necessary for expanded participation.

- Establish a formal or informal mentor/sponsor program to foster employee professional development as management control is reduced.

- Incorporate enhanced information technology and offer training for necessary skills acquisition.

Integrated Infrastructures

Most organizations that decide to implement empowerment have also begun or have been implementing other related initiatives, such as quality, reengineering, customer-focus, teamwork, etc. In such cases, an empowerment infrastructure is best designed as an "integrated infrastructure" which includes principles and practices of the other initiatives. As we have previously discussed, empowerment is the "anchor initiative" which is common to all of the others in terms of structure, systems, and practices.

> After winning a major quality award, Global Technical Systems decided to aggressively institute teaming, diversity, and empowerment. Each of the initiatives were pursued separately. Significant investment and sustained effort were committed to the teaming and empowerment efforts, but less visible support and accountability measures were involved in the diversity effort. In reviewing the lack of success of the former two initiatives, the leadership decided that employees seemed to be working less well together, in spite of the greater autonomy. The CEO decided that the "quality of work life" for *all* employees was the source of the problem. Instead of focusing on separate support systems for each of the initiatives, the organization designed an integrated diversity, empowerment, and teaming infrastructure. This was a major step in having employees see the connection among these initiatives, as well as bringing the diversity initiative into their mainstream thrusts.

In the next chapter, we discuss the relationships among quality, empowerment, and diversity. Understanding these relationships provides the knowledge base necessary to design an integrated infrastructure. We also illustrate how empowerment is the anchor initiative which makes diversity and quality inseparable.

152

CHAPTER FOURTEEN

QUALITY, EMPOWERMENT, AND DIVERSITY

This chapter is intended to show the relationship between quality, empowerment, and diversity. The discussion of quality is not intended to be a repeat of the well-known tenets of quality, such as TQM. It is intended to focus on the mindset we bring to how we perform our jobs. You have probably surmised by now that we believe a person's mental attitude toward serving and learning are key to having a "quality state of mind." This state of mind, in turn, leads to the most effective utilization of the quality techniques, methodologies, and metrics. Without this way of thinking, quality is simply a *process* of continually creating a never-ending sequence of corrective measures in an attempt to meet a performance standard. At best, this process is continuous improvement, but not quality as an institutionalized way of thinking and doing.

In truth, quality *begins* with a mindset which *anticipates* what serves a customer without the necessity of being told or the experience of breakdown. It literally requires continually seeing the world through the eyes of one's customer. The process of implementation, sourced from this mindset, is synonymous with what we define as empowerment. Therefore, quality and empowerment are inseparable.

Diversity focuses on differences. Differences in the way people are, the way people think, and the way people create systems and processes to produce products, goods, and services. The extent to which the expression of differences is accepted and encouraged is probably proportional to the extent to which empowerment is effectively implemented. In this sense, diversity and empowerment are also inseparable.

Four Corollaries of Quality

If the quality of a product is synonymous with the quality of performance of its producers, then consistent competitive quality is not possible without empowered employees. This relationship is summarized by four simple, yet powerful, corollaries of quality.

1) **"Do it right the first time."**

2) **"Should it have been done at all?**

3) **"There is no such thing as an honest mistake."**

4) **"If it ain't broke, fix it."**

Each of these corollaries involves people to a greater extent than they do systems, although the two are *always* interconnected. In spite of the fact that most organizations view lack of quality as primarily a systems issue, we would suggest that the greatest contributor is our lack of appreciation and/or investment in the development of people; specifically, their personal empowerment.

Do it Right the First Time

"Do it right the first time" is probably most identified with Phil Crosby. When this slogan is truly embraced and

practiced, it has the potential to change your life. For example, if a typist or computer specialist suggests to co-workers that no document or manuscript should be revised more than once after being typed the first time, this forces each of the co-workers to produce a more complete copy the first time; thereby, reducing time, energy, and effort by both co-workers and typist. It forces one to be in intimate contact with the customer *before* the product or service is produced, since doing it right means meeting or exceeding customer requirements.

Eventually, this principle begins to apply everywhere in your life, whether painting the house with the utmost preparation, shopping with a well thought-through list, arranging a series of errands to maximize the success of each, etc. Even most meetings have to be held only once if the necessary preparations for time, information, and materials are properly handled in advance. This is a very powerful principle that forces one to more effectively organize his or her life and is obviously the foundation for life management.

Should it Have Been Done at All?

"Should it have been done at all?" forces us to stop and think how we not only prioritize our activities, but spend time doing things which are unnecessary (because of low priority or outdatedness) or could have been delegated through mentoring. The quality of our time could be more effectively utilized by asking three questions daily: 1) "Could someone else do it?", 2) "Is it really someone else's job?", and 3) "Is it necessary to be done at all?" One of the most common examples of this principle is the unchecked proliferation of paper, both in quantity of written materials and/or the length of a document; especially since we have laser printers.

155

Another common office example is storing useless information in computer memory which will never be used or is of no interest to anyone in an organization. "The memory storage is there, why not use it!"

This corollary is perhaps best captured by the Pareto Principle which states that "80% of the important results in an organization are produced by 20% of the time, energy, and effort of employees." Where customer focus and reengineering exists, employees are continually eliminating outdated processes. One of the best ways to utilize this principle to derive the greatest quality usage of your time is to make a "short" to-do list daily with each item prioritized in terms of "must absolutely do myself," "must mentor someone else to do," and "must delegate to someone." Ultimately, only those items in the first category should be on your list.

There is No Such Thing as an Honest Mistake

"There is no such thing as an honest mistake" is a very challenging corollary, probably because most people *believe* there are honest mistakes which they feel they had little or nothing to do with. We do not *believe* this. Therefore, we do not live consistent with the unconscious expectation that "honest mistakes" will occur. What we are suggesting here is that what people believe, even unconsciously, frequently or infrequently occurs.

To get a better sense of what we are suggesting involves reminding ourselves of two important realizations of how life works. One, what you believe is what you expect to occur. Two, belief coupled with expectation creates what happens in your life. Conclusion, if you believe "honest mistakes happen," then all you need to do is, retrospectively, scan your life or more importantly your organization, and we are confident you will find a series of "unfortunate incidents" that could be understood by everyone as honest mistakes. Furthermore, you can be assured that they will occur endlessly, with frequency!

Organizations that manufacture highly dangerous materials or that are involved in activities that could easily jeopardize the health of their employees, understand this corollary perfectly. They typically display large billboards publicizing their record of safety for "x" number of days. The objective is to create a "safety consciousness," which is to have its employees adopt a mindset that *through proper precautions, mistakes rarely, if ever, happen.* If you adopt this mindset, then when and if a mistake occurs, you begin to observe the incident as a valuable feedback source about how people and systems are working. Mistakes (even honest ones) are often indicative of necessary improvement in one of four areas:

i)   Planning

ii)   Prioritizing

iii) Procedure

iv)   Preparation

All four of these areas involve the performance of employees, not solely in terms of methodology and skills, but in terms of the efficient usage of time, energy, and effort. Procedure is the acknowledgement that there *is* a most efficient and effective system of doing things in an organization, which fits best the personalities involved. As always, the final measure is the quality with which internal and external clients or customers are served.

Another elusive aspect of this corollary is that honest mistakes rarely, if ever, look the same. Therefore, they do not immediately reveal themselves as a pattern of general breakdown or relaxation of rigor in one of the four areas above. Only upon close inspection of a given mistake does one begin to observe something of a more *general* nature involving people and/or procedure.

For example, an excellent producing employee who always appears to be overwhelmed and occasionally but systematically makes honest mistakes, may have fundamental difficulties in the areas of prioritizing and planning. Their outstanding output is often used as a veil to divert attention away from these areas of difficulty. Whenever a series of honest mistakes is examined and addressed in terms of one (or more) of the four performance areas cited above, an individual (or an organization) is provided the opportunity to establish a quantum jump in quality.

If it Ain't Broke, Fix It

"If it ain't broke, fix it" is a corollary which makes the basic assumption, "There is *always* an improved way of delivering a product or service." Quality is a dynamic process of maximizing productivity and workmanship within the present time frame. Therefore, a quality product or service today will not be equivalent to the same quality of that product or service one month or one year from now. The slogan of an automobile manufacturer captures the spirit of this dynamic element, *"The relentless pursuit of perfection."* The first implication of this slogan is that quality is not a goal, but an ongoing process of improvement. This impetus for improvement is continual customer-encouraged feedback.

158

This corollary is a requirement, in order to remain at the cutting edge of creativity. This attitude sets the pace for others to follow and usually mimic. In fact, the most revealing characteristic of an organization that is not operating according to this corollary is one that appears to copy what the quality organizations are *doing*. This practice may appear to work in the short term, but will *not* sustain quality in the long term. Quality, as a state of mind, is the source of doing things in a way that produces exceptional excellence. The *essence* of quality is not a methodology, product, or service. These are the manifestations of quality. It is vital to understand this distinction, or an organization will never achieve true quality as an institutionalized way of operating.

Quality begins with encouraging, expecting, and training people to think a certain way about what they do. It appeals to something inherent in every individual, and that is the desire to express their full potential in an activity for which they have an interest and the mental and physical skills. This is the essence of empowerment! The key becomes how to unblock those "invisible barriers" that seem to prevent such unlimited expression. We are back to education and training as ongoing integral parts of an organization's operation to ensure consistent expanding performance. We now understand that the most important part of this corollary is the systematic process of "*fixing* the creative potential of people" even when it ain't broke or more organizationally stated, realizing expanded personal and professional growth. When your mind expands to *realize* what you are capable of doing, you will produce it!

A quote which summarizes best the requirements for quality within an organization is the following from a *Business Week Magazine* article, "The Push for Quality," June 8, 1987:

"Managing for quality means nothing less than a sweeping overhaul in corporate culture, a radical shift in management philosophy, and a permanent commitment at all levels of the organization to seek continuous improvement."

In an article published in the *Wall Street Journal* (October 2, 1991), Peter F. Drucker pointed out that major Japanese corporations were adding a new twist to this corollary, *"If it ain't broke, break it."* The new strategy was to begin the replacement for a new product the day it is sold to the public. And the way to maintain dominance in the marketplace while development of the replacement product was occurring was to institutionalize Zero Defect Management (ZDM). ZDM establishes a higher level of quality than does TQM, which has inherently an acceptable level of error of 10%. If this strategy is successful, Drucker states that Japanese corporate leaders believe by 1995, they will be 10 years ahead of competitive markets in the area of quality. Obviously, Motorola's Sigma Six program is a response to this prediction. In essence, Sigma Six's ultimate goal is to achieve 3.4 defects per million.

Diversity and Empowerment

We recently got an urgent telephone call from one of our clients. The manager of a manufacturing business unit indicated that they had purposely sought to create vertical, as well as, horizonal teams. What they had not paid particular attention to was the fact that the business unit consisted of 50% women and 50% men, 70% non-managers and 30% managers/ supervisors, 49% minorities and 51% non-minorities, and 49% non-exempt and 51% exempt. Less than a month after implementing challenging but standard teaming processes, productivity was going down rather than going up. Finally, the highly charged but ignored issues of diversity cited above began to emerge. Employees who had all along harbored feelings of inequity, began to speak out. The conclusion was obvious, the extent to which teaming was going to be successful was dependent upon how effectively issues of diversity were resolved. We were asked to create a seminar which would help them resolve issues of differences, so that they could concentrate on the teaming effort.

This example illustrates the fact that diversity and empowerment are inseparable where the work force composition is different or bring differences to the work process — assuming that the expression of differences is tolerated and possibly encouraged. This statement applies to any work force, although it is more pronounced in the U.S. because of the many dimensions of diversity which naturally exist. Even a group who is similar by race and/or sex is diverse, though fewer in dimensions.

Dimensions of Diversity

The various dimensions of diversity can be classified as *human, cultural,* and *systems as* outlined below:

Human diversity is characterized by virtue of the physicality or life experience of an individual. These include:

- Race
- Sex
- Differently-Abled
- Marital/Family Status
- Sexual Orientation
- Ethnicity
- Age
- Military Experience

Cultural diversity is characterized by fundamental beliefs, attitudes, assumptions, values, and personal characteristics. These include:

- Language
- Learning Style
- Gender
- Historical Differences
- Cross-Cultural Relationship/ Communication
- Polychronic/ Monochronic

- Religion
- Workstyle
- Classism/Elitism
- Ethics/Values
- Lifestyle
- Family-Friendly Practices
- High/Low Context
- Teaming

Systems diversity is characterized by the integration of organizational structures and management operating systems where differences are involved or implicit. These include:

- Teamwork
- Innovation
- Reengineering
- Strategic Alliances

- Empowerment
- Quality
- Education
- Corporate Acquisitions

Human diversity principally involves the issue of human equality relating to the presumed inherent superiority/ inferiority of individuals based primarily upon physically distinguishing characteristics. Cultural diversity involves issues of ethnocentrism. The human tendency to assume that one's culture and way of life is superior to others. Systems diversity deals with systems-thinking. The ability to recognize the connections among "different-looking" systems and to be open and receptive to their *integration*. Of the three classifications, systems diversity is least recognized and consciously utilized as a diversity advantage. We cited "team diversity" in the various team descriptions in Table 1, pg 63.

162

We also acknowledged "empowerment diversity," when we encouraged the full use of the empowerment continuum in Figure 1, pg 8. These examples are the essence of systems diversity.

The example about teaming which we used at the beginning of the section on Diversity and Empowerment (pg 160) is a good illustration of how an attempt to implement systems diversity automatically involves issues of both human and cultural diversity. Thus, we might also conclude that issues of diversity become more pronounced as an organization shifts from hierarchy to high-involvement. Hierarchy requires management decision-making as the major operational mode whereas high-involvement encourages mutual resolution and consensus for operational success.

Cross-Cultural Diversity and Empowerment

As the shift occurs from transnational organizations (independently operating worldwide business units) to global organizations (integrated worldwide operation) international cultural diversity becomes increasingly important. Besides the unique nuances of doing business in a given country, diversity is the key factor in the successful operation of global teams. Avon Products, Inc. recognized the similarities of the countries comprising the "Latin Belt" — Italy, France, Spain, Portugal, Mexico, and the countries of South America. This realization led to a global marketing strategy which integrated the successful efforts from each of these countries. This is an example of utilizing the combination of systems diversity (teamwork) with cultural diversity (national cultures) as a competitive advantage.

CHAPTER FIFTEEN

ROADMAP TO EMPOWERMENT

The following pages outline a flow diagram for achieving an empowered organization. We have modeled empowerment as a three-phase program. The first phase is *preparation*, the second phase is *implementation*, and the third phase is *nirvana*. Although we believe the sequences suggested for each phase are best for an empowerment initiative, what is more important is that each element is achieved in the overall process.

Preparation and Implementation

The elements of the preparation and implementation phases have been discussed throughout this text, with the exception of the Leadership Executive Assessment and the Organizational Empowerment Assessment in the second phase. The former is a 360° assessment of each member of the senior leadership team. That is, an assessment of themselves and a comparative assessment by their chosen reporting managers and/or employees. The results of the assessment are ideally presented and discussed as a private two to three hour consulting session. The result is a plan for improving those areas perceived by managers and/or employees as requiring improvement. When this session is conducted by a skillful facilitator, the change in an executive can be profound.

A COMPREHENSIVE EMPOWERMENT PROGRAM

FIRST PHASE
(Preparation)

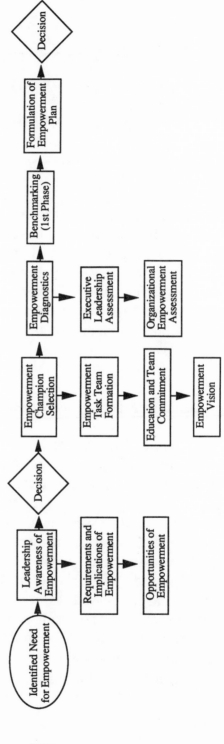

166

SECOND PHASE
(Implementation)

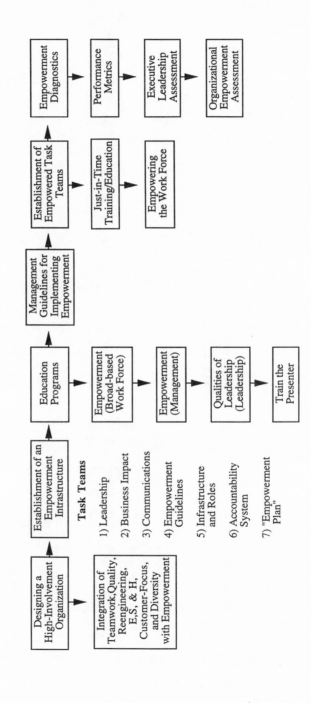

THIRD PHASE
(Nirvana)

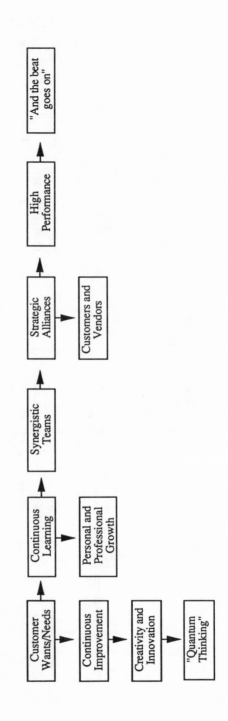

Empowerment

The Organizational Empowerment Assessment is an instrument which quantitatively measures the relative extent of the Organizational Support System and Individual and Team Empowerment. That is, it gives quantitative measures of the two solid arrows on pg 4. This instrument also measures the personal empowerment of an employee, identifies the most important areas for empowerment improvement, and serves as a baseline for future measurement of success.

The sequence of the Education Programs cited in the second phase are respectively designed for the non-management work force, managers and supervisors, and leadership. They are best performed simultaneously, but leadership should be one of the initial groups. This series is the initial introduction to empowerment and how it is implemented according to the philosophy of this text. The other elements of phase two have been discussed elsewhere or are obvious in their descriptions.

Although customers are the center of attention in instituting empowerment in the first two phases, they also drive the cyclic process of phase three. Nirvana, as a description, is meant to characterize the ideal state of operation. As a new service or product is generated, as a result of customers' wants and/or needs, the sequence of phase three is played out to institutionalized high performance and circles back to the customer wants and needs box — and the beat goes on. This cycle always begins and ends with the customer as the driving force for continuous improvement, creativity and innovation, and quantum change, either in meeting a want or anticipating a need.

Quantum-Thinking

Eventually, the cycle of continuous improvement of a service or product runs its course. Forward-thinking organizations recognize that at this point, what is needed is the next generation service or product. A higher level of creativity and innovation are required than was necessary for continuous improvement. Organizations that discourage, *in practice*, creative and innovative employees are often *forced* into coming up with something new or copying the latest service or product of forward-thinking organizations. Such organizations continually border on extinction.

Achieving high performance (pg 11) is the *entre* into the game of business, particularly from a global perspective. The competitive lifetime of a product or service is becoming shorter and shorter. One question is, "How does a business remain competitive?" However, a more powerful question is "How does a business stay *ahead* of competition?" The answer is "quantum-thinking."

Quantum-thinking is the ability of the mind to function at a higher order of creativity. This natural ability is achieved by the systematic development of six critical skills:

1)   Personal and professional mastery

2)   Creative synthesis

3)   Intuition

4)   Context integration

5)   Hyper-accelerated information processing

6)   Mastery of context

Organizations that capture, nourish, and fully encourage these characteristics in a critical core of employees will have such a decided advantage, that competition will be the least of their problems. Each of these six elements are discussed, in turn, below.

Personal and professional mastery is the result of in-depth self-introspection coupled with self-motivated continual learning. Personal mastery involves the willingness to move beyond self-imposed barriers to discover one's *true* potential. Professional mastery is achieved by the continual absorption of new information *and* the creative integration of that information within one's existing knowledge base.   The combination of the two is self-mastery. The breakthrough experience to self-mastery is the realization and acceptance that change is not only a necessity, but an opportunity for creative adaptation.   Therefore, the confidence to create whatever is required, at whatever level necessary, is a given. The ultimate realization of self-mastery is that, given the requisite competencies, one has the power, in large part, to create one's reality.

Creative synthesis is the ability to create at a "meta" level relative to the existing knowledge base. This ability requires an expansive base of information and knowledge. The critical experience is freely accessing one's creative capacity by the unlimited exploration of one's creative consciousness. The opening of this doorway is the key to the mastery of creative synthesis. Personal transformation is an inherent part of the creative process.   The fear accompanying unpredictable transformative change is the greatest barrier to mastery of this skill. As Picasso stated, "The act of creation is simultaneously the act of destruction." This skill is learned by using an array of creative transformative processes. The creativity model used for these processes is based upon the assumption that the source of creative inspiration is beyond the mind.

Intuition is the process of experiencing "instantaneous perception" of insight, information, knowing, or creativity. It is sometimes referred to as the sixth sense. Development of this skill is based, most of all, on trust in one's self. That is, the willingness to be cognitively receptive to the spontaneous reception of information with the least amount of self-doubt. We each experience intuition in unique ways — by seeing, feeling, hearing, and knowing. The practice of "quieting the mind" is usually the prelude to intuitive perception. Each of us has a natural propensity for experiencing intuition in a unique way. And on many occasions we have! For example, you may have experienced an instantaneous feeling from nowhere, followed by a "complete perception" that was not logically deduced. This complete perception integrates bits and pieces of data and information such that a complete situation is revealed, although total proof is lacking. Depending on the nature of the intuitive insight, it must often be balanced with rationality before being put into practice.

Context integration is the ability to grasp the "big picture" with the least amount of data or information. It is the ability to perceive the whole system from the intuitive understanding of how a limited number of parts are interrelated. Context integration goes beyond systems-thinking in that it involves an understanding of how a given set of parts or components can belong to several different contexts or systems. These contexts, comprised of similar components, are by definition interrelated. Thus, interrelated contexts provide the opportunity for the creation of a new superordinate context. This new superordinate context is the basis for a new breakthrough performance, product, or service. For example teamwork, quality, and reengineering originally appeared to be different performance initiatives (contexts). However, upon examination of each, we observe that they all have, in common, self-management, expanded responsibility and accountability, and continuous-learning (contents). The new superordinate context is High Performance.

Hyper-accelerated information processing is the ability of the human mind to process data and information at hyper-accelerated speeds. This ability involves a combination of speed cognition and holistic knowing. Using this skill requires a knowledge base of the subject to which it is applied. It requires the hyper-accelerated integration of new information, which expands one's knowledge base of that subject, since interrelated data is information, and creatively integrated information is new knowledge. As new information is integrated into an existing context, it necessarily modifies and transforms the existing content. As a subject (product or service) becomes mature, the continual integration of new information quite often results in the spontaneous creation of a new context. The breakthrough experience in acquiring this skill is receptivity to the rapid accumulation of information without the necessity of evaluating how it might change one's present reality. Quite often, the attachment to one's present reality *is* the major barrier to mastering this skill.

Mastery of context is the ability to simultaneously be committed to a project and detached from the process or the outcome. It is the ability to be committed without investment. This skill is captured by the expression "being in the world but not of (or controlled by) the world." For example, if one is *committed* to creating the next generation work force performance paradigm, one has to be totally detached from *all* the present popular initiatives. Once detachment is achieved, one can operate within or beyond the present paradigm in a centered manner. Literally any idea can be considered in presented or modified form in a way which focuses on the objective without regard to what presently exists. In general, the ability to operate "meta" to a paradigm is mastery.

Nirvana Continued

The objective for empowered high performance organizations is to continually operate in phase three. Following the flow diagram on page 168, the necessity to meet a customer need or want is continuous-learning. This learning may involve a personal expansion process as described in quantum-thinking or the mastery of a new technical skill. The attitude is one of receptive dynamic growth. That is, life is a continuous process of learning where feedback for improvement is a guide to engage the process. Then we begin to understand the Japanese concept of *kaizen* — continuous improvement through an attitude of voluntary continuous self-improvement. It is a process with endless milestones.

Synergistic teams were discussed in Chapter Nine. Since such teams and individuals operate in a self-directed manner, they are often in direct contact with the customer. The establishment of a committed long-term customer/vendor relationship is a strategic alliance. Such alliances require significant overlap of philosophies and values. They are alliances with a "no divorce clause." These are established after a long period of mutual discussion and experience. They also begin to approach the Japanese *keiretsus*.

The culmination of the three-phase process (for the present) is a high performance organization as described on page 10. This offers both the challenge and the opportunity for forward-thinking organizations for the remainder of this decade.

BIBLIOGRAPHY

1) Harry S. Dent, Jr., **The Great Boom Ahead**, Hyperion, New York, NY 10017, 1993.

2) John E. Rehfeld, **Alchemy of a Leader**, John Wiley & Sons, Inc., New York, NY 10010, 1994.

3) Richard S. Wellins, William C. Byham, Jeanne M. Wilson, **Empowered Teams**, Jossey-Bass Publishers, San Francisco, CA 94104, 1991.

4) Peter M. Senge, **The Fifth Discipline**, Doubleday Currency, New York, NY 10103, 1990.

5) Joseph Campbell, **The Power of Myth**, The HighBridge Company, St. Paul, MN 55114, 1990.

6) Michael Hammer and James Champy, **Reengineering the Corporation**, HarperBusiness, New York, NY 10022, 1993.

7) Elizabeth Kübler-Ross, **On Death and Dying**, Macmillan Publishing Company, New York, NY 10022, 1970.

8) Peter Block, **Stewardship**, Berrett-Koehler Publishers, San Francisco, CA 94104, 1993.

9) Judith F. Vogt and Kenneth L. Murrell, **Empowerment in Organizations**, University Associates, Inc., San Diego, CA 92121, 1990.

10) Edward E. Lawler III, **The Ultimate Advantage**, Jossey-Bass Publishers, San Francisco, CA 94104, 1992.

Empowerment Vocabulary

Empowerment is the performance capacity of an individual, a team, or an organization.

Management by Empowerment is a management system designed to optimize organizational performance through the extensive participation of employees.

Personal Responsibility is the willingness to be the *principal source* of the results which occur in your life.

Personal Accountability is the willingness to *own* the results which occur in your life.

Personal Empowerment is an *internally-derived capacity* to continually perform to your maximum ability.

Delegation is the granting of authority with decision-making power within clearly defined guidelines.

Coaching is the interactive process of facilitating the expanded performance of an employee or co-worker.

Mentoring is the interactive process of overseeing and guiding the success of an employee or co-worker (and may or may not involve coaching).

Management/Supervision/Sponsorship is the process of overseeing the performance of a project or task to successful completion (and may or may not result in expanded empowerment).

A Commitment is a binding agreement with an individual and/or group to accomplish a task, project, or service.

INDEX

About the Authors:

Dr. William A. Guillory is the CEO and Founder of Innovations Consulting International, Inc. He has presented over 2,000 seminars throughout corporate America, Europe, Mexico, and Canada. He has facilitated seminars for over 150 corporations, including Diversity, Empowerment, Creativity and Innovation, and Leadership programs for the senior management of American Airlines, Avon Products, Inc., Eastman Kodak Company, Electronic Data Systems, Martin Marietta Corporation, Sandia National Laboratories, Rohm and Haas Company, and Texas Instruments.

Dr. Guillory is an authority on diversity and empowerment. He is the author of two books on personal transformation, *Realizations* and *It's All an Illusion*. He is also a member of NTL. His distinguished awards and appointments include an Alfred P. Sloan Fellowship, an Alexander von Humboldt appointment at the University of Frankfurt, a Ralph Metcalf Chair at Marquette University, and the Chancellor's Distinguished Lectureship at the University of California at Berkeley. He has been a keynote speaker for national and international organizations including *The International Chapter of the Society for Human Resource Management* and *The Institute for Management Studies*.

Dr. Guillory facilitates seminars on the following topics: *Diversity — A Global Perspective; Valuing and Managing Diversity; Empowerment; Creativity and Innovation; Qualities of Leadership;* and *Quantum Thinking*.

Prior to founding Innovations, Dr. Guillory was a physical chemist of international renown, receiving his Ph.D. from the University of California at Berkeley. He has lived, studied, and lectured in England, France, Germany, Japan, Switzerland,

Poland, and China. He is the author of over one hundred publications and several books on the applications of lasers in chemistry and was the Chairman of the Department of Chemistry at the University of Utah. Dr. Guillory founded Innovations in 1985 following a period of intense personal growth which led to a career change to individual and organizational transformation.

Linda Galindo is the President and Co-Founder of Innovations International, Inc. She is a Senior Consultant and Facilitator and has presented over 1,500 seminars throughout corporate America. Ms. Galindo has been widely recognized for her outstanding presentations and her leadership in business. She was named as one of the top ten outstanding business women in the state of Utah by *Utah Business Magazine*. She has been recognized with an "Outstanding Presentation" award from *The American Society for Training and Development*, and was also recognized by the Salt Lake Area Chamber of Commerce with a "Pathfinder Award" for her history of work to further the development of women in business.

Ms. Galindo has facilitated presentations for over 100 hospitals and healthcare organizations, including VA Medical Centers, Brim Healthcare, Intermountain Health Care, and the Mayo Clinic, as well as Eastman Kodak, Electronic Data Systems, Trammell Crow, and Texas Instruments.

Ms. Galindo facilitates seminars on the following: *Managing and Valuing Diversity; Empowering the Work Force; Insights for Success; Responsibility, Accountability, and Empowerment;* and *The Human Aspects of Selling.*

Ms. Galindo writes a monthly column for *Network Magazine* on Personal Empowerment.